T0311400

WORK PSYCHOLOGY
THE BASICS

Work Psychology: The Basics provides an accessible, jargon-free introduction to the fundamental principles of work and occupational psychology. Covering key theories and models in this dynamic area, it offers a solid understanding of both academic theory and practical applications.

The book follows the structure of the British Psychological Society curriculum for Masters courses, exploring psychological assessment at work, learning, training and development, wellbeing at work, work design, organisational change and development, and leadership, engagement and motivation. These core topics are supplemented by deep dives into the development of the discipline, research and practice in the field, and suggestions for the future of work psychology. Giving a detailed look into the world of work, it answers questions such as: *Can we accurately select people for jobs? How can work positively and negatively affect mental and physical health? How can we motivate people in the workplace? What makes a good leader?* It also explores issues around types of research and what effective research looks like in this area.

Supported by a helpful guide on the routes to chartership in the UK and working in the area, as well as a glossary of key terms and suggestions for further reading, this is the ideal introductory text for students. It will also interest those looking to understand the subject more generally and complete training in the area.

Dr. Laura Dean is a chartered psychologist with the British Psychological Society and a registered health psychologist with the

UK Health and Care Professions Council (HCPC). She is the programme director for the Stage 1 Occupational Psychology programme at the University of Sheffield, UK. Her research interests are focused on equality and diversity issues, particularly the effects of social class and the disadvantages faced by autistic people.

Fran Cousans is an independent business psychologist with over a decade of experience in consulting and academia. She specializes in working with organisations to help them assess and select the best talent and is a university tutor of quantitative research methods and occupational psychology.

The Basics Series

The Basics is a highly successful series of accessible guidebooks which provide an overview of the fundamental principles of a subject area in a jargon-free and undaunting format.

Intended for students approaching a subject for the first time, the books both introduce the essentials of a subject and provide an ideal springboard for further study. With over 50 titles spanning subjects from artificial intelligence (AI) to women's studies, *The Basics* are an ideal starting point for students seeking to understand a subject area.

Each text comes with recommendations for further study and gradually introduces the complexities and nuances within a subject.

For a full list of titles in this series, please visit www.routledge.com/The-Basics/book-series/B

WORK PSYCHOLOGY

THE BASICS

Laura Dean and Fran Cousans

Routledge
Taylor & Francis Group

LONDON AND NEW YORK

Designed cover image: © Getty Images

First published 2024
by Routledge
4 Park Square, Milton Park, Abingdon, Oxon OX14 4RN

and by Routledge
605 Third Avenue, New York, NY 10158

Routledge is an imprint of the Taylor & Francis Group, an informa business

British Library Cataloguing-in-Publication Data
A catalogue record for this book is available from the British Library

Library of Congress Cataloging-in-Publication Data
Names: Dean, Laura (Psychologist), author. | Cousans, Frances, author.
Title: Work psychology : the basics / Dr. Laura Dean and Frances Cousans.
Description: Abingdon, Oxon ; New York, NY : Routledge, 2024. | Includes
bibliographical references and index. | Summary: "Work Psychology: The Basics
provides an accessible, jargon-free introduction to the fundamental principles
of work and occupational psychology. Covering key theories and models in this
dynamic area, it offers a solid understanding of both academic theory and practical
applications"—Provided by publisher.
Identifiers: LCCN 2023018150 (print) | LCCN 2023018151 (ebook) |
ISBN 9781138048966 (paperback) | ISBN 9781138048942 (hardback) |
ISBN 9781315169880 (ebook)
Subjects: LCSH: Work—Psychological aspects. | Psychology, Industrial.
Classification: LCC BF481 .D38 2024 (print) | LCC BF481 (ebook) | DDC 158.7—
dc23/eng/20230509
LC record available at https://lccn.loc.gov/2023018150
LC ebook record available at https://lccn.loc.gov/2023018151

ISBN: 978-1-138-04894-2 (hbk)
ISBN: 978-1-138-04896-6 (pbk)
ISBN: 978-1-315-16988-0 (ebk)

DOI: 10.4324/9781315169880

Typeset in Bembo
by codeMantra

CONTENTS

THE DEVELOPMENT OF WORK PSYCHOLOGY

This chapter focuses on establishing the context of work psychology by explaining the changing patterns of work and describing the role of work psychology in supporting both individuals and organisations. The chapter begins by examining how work psychology evolved to meet the changing needs of organisations from selection and assessment to supporting wellbeing at work. It then goes on to explain current issues in work psychology and how research and practice can be applied to issues such as unemployment, the ageing workforce and the digital age.

WHAT IS WORK PSYCHOLOGY

Work psychology is a broad term which is used to describe the different ways in which psychological principles and practices are used in the workplace by practitioners who may have a range of different titles and specialise in different areas. It is worth noting that globally names and terminology differ. In North America work psychology is typically split into industrial and organisational psychology. Industrial psychology considers issues more akin to human resource management elsewhere in the world, such as selection and assessment, training and appraisal. Organisational psychology is more person focused and looks at topics such as leadership, motivation and

DOI: 10.4324/9781315169880-1

wellbeing. In the UK these two broad areas are brought together under the title occupational psychology. Occupational psychology also incorporates aspects of social psychology, health psychology and ergonomics. The title Occupational Psychologist is protected in the UK. How that title can be gained is covered in the working practices part of this chapter.

A range of professional bodies oversee work psychology practice and research. The Society for Industrial and Organizational Psychology (SIOP) was formed in 1945 and is a division of the American Psychological Association (APA). Covering most of Europe is the European Association of Work and Organizational Psychology (EAWOP), formed in 1991 in order to share knowledge across Europe. It now works much more widely than this since the Alliance for Organizational Psychology brought together SIOP and EAWOP along with the International Association for Applied Psychology (IAAP). This umbrella organisation subsequently incorporated the Canadian Society for Industrial and Organizational Psychology (CSIOP) and now is the largest work psychology body in the world. The UK has two key professional organisations. The British Psychological Society (BPS) regulates the content and quality of training in universities as well as conferring chartership in all branches of psychology, whilst the Health and Care Professions Council (HCPC) acts as the regulator for psychologists once they have become Chartered. There are a range of other notable work psychology organisations including: Australian Psychological Society: Organisational Psychology; Chinese Psychological Society Division of Industrial Psychology; Global Organization for Humanitarian Work Psychology; and Society for Industrial and Organisational Psychology of South Africa. Most nations don't have a discrete society/division for work psychology though, and often it is subsumed under general psychology societies.

This book explores the five main topic areas as dictated by the BPS for master's qualifications in occupational psychology taking a chapter on each. These are: psychological assessment at work; learning, training and development; wellbeing at work; work design, organisational change and development; and leadership, engagement and motivation. The final chapters look specifically at research and practice in work psychology and the future of work psychology.

HISTORY OF WORK AND OF WORK PSYCHOLOGY

The early 20th century represented a real start to what might be called work psychology now. This emerging field came from changes to the way in which work was completed; increasing industrialisation and global war in the shape of the First World War coupled with the devastation caused by the Spanish Flu epidemic led to shifts in who was working and how that work was completed. During this period there was increasing polarisation of nations in terms of how technologically developed they were, their GDPs, birth and death rates. Work psychology emerged in some developed nations. There was already a tradition of psychology in Germany and the United States, and the United Kingdom was an early adopter and developer of the more applied form of work psychology. Consequently, early research comes mainly from these nations and it is only within the last two decades that the field has opened up in less industrialised nations, still being comparatively unknown throughout Africa and parts of Asia.

Early psychology work focused particularly on efficiencies in the workplace or on removing physical health problems resulting from work. In the United States the first PhD specifically in the field of work psychology was awarded to Lillian Galbreth in 1915. She used the latest technology in film to study workers' movements and explore how they could be made more efficient. This technique became known as 'time and motion' studies and was widely disliked by employees and critiqued as descriptive of process rather than exploring employees' understanding of their own work organisation and process. It proved an effective technique for creating efficiencies in more manual and repetitive tasks though. Improving efficiency and overall productivity was also a feature of the research conducted by the National Institute of Industrial Psychology (NIIP) established in the UK in 1921. This organisation came more from a medical approach, however. It was funded by the Medical Research Council and resulted from the early work of the Industrial Fatigue Health Board (1918) and the Industrial Health Research Board (1928). The NIIP focused on how human factors impact productivity, drawing together both psychological and physiological aspects. The institute explored issues such as job analysis and psychometrics as well as careers guidance and recruitment and selection issues. This early work was accelerated by the demands of the First World War. In the US, work psychologists looked at issues such as military selection, and the army employed what were then termed Industrial Psychologists to develop what became known as the Army Alpha and Army Beta tests. These were psychometric tools for recruits who could and could not read respectively, to ensure each was assigned the most appropriate roles according their abilities. Even then work psychologists explored a broad range of issues. For example, working on improved ergonomic design of aeroplane cockpits to reduce cognitive load on pilots as well as efficiencies in physical movement within the space.

In the inter-war period, the German military continued to use the psychometric principles already established in recruitment, and work psychologists built a three-day assessment for aspiring officers. Suprisingly, at this stage the techniques weren't widely transferred to industrial settings, and interest even in other militaries waned. The civilian work psychologists advising these militaries returned to their day jobs. Some experiments began moving out into real work settings at this time. The now famous Hawthorne studies were conducted during the 1920s though it wasn't until the 1960s when there was a large shift of psychologists out of laboratories and into the field. These studies took place at the Hawthorne Works, an electric plant in the USA. They are famous for the finding that employees' productivity was impacted by the mere presence of, or interest from, psychologists, and so by default work psychology would need to be more subtle in how studies involved humans as participants. In fact, the same point had been made several times earlier, for example in published work from the NIIP, but the researcher Elton Mayo is credited with the naming of the phenomenon as the Hawthorne effect.

At the outbreak of the Second World War there was again interest in employing work psychologists to help with recruitment. In the UK the NIIP seconded their psychologists to the navy to design and deliver psychometric assessment tests. Progressive Matrices tests were developed and given to three million recruits. In the early stages of the war there was much criticism of how the UK army were led. Traditionally, commissioned officers were drawn from the upper classes. The War Office Selection Boards were established and used personality measures as well as intelligence tests and observations of applicants. Throughout this period work psychologists focused on quantitative improvements: making efficiencies and widely employing statistical techniques. The early history of work psychology is widely tied to developments in statistical practice with psychologists creating a range of new techniques now in wide use.

In the post-war period some of this learning was brought back into businesses, more so in the USA than elsewhere. Large organisations such as Sears, IBM and AT&T began employing work psychologists to build their selection processes and help with work problems. In the UK the civil service took forward the ideas used in military recruitment and are now one of the largest recruiters of Occupational Psychologists. Changes in social and political ideas in this period led to a greater interest in diversity and equality issues in the workplace from the 1960s onwards. In the USA this was driven by the civil rights movement, across Europe the focus was more on gender-based discrimination. The field of work psychology was still led from medical perspectives in the UK largely though. From 1964–67 the Medical Research Council conducted a review which argued that the field of work psychology was of national importance and should be funded. Consequently, the Social and Applied Psychology Unit (SAPU) was set up at the University of Sheffield in 1968 as a research centre (this later became the Institute of Work Psychology (IWP)). Their early research continued the theme of efficiencies in the workplace however the routes to understanding how to create efficiencies became more diverse. They explored attitudes, motivation, learning and decision-making in the workplace. The unit aimed to influence psychology academics to focus more on practical issues and encouraged the BPS to produce a journal which focused on occupational issues. In 1975 the *Journal of Occupational Psychology* was launched, which later became the highly regarded *Journal of Occupational and Organizational Psychology* (JOOP).

From the 1970s onwards the overall structure of the profession began to become more concrete. Until this point it had covered virtually any problem in the workplace. In 1975 SAPU created the first master's course in occupational psychology, which meant the BPS began establishing curriculum areas and defining what it meant to be an occupational psychologist: a practical training route was established. As of 2023 there are over twenty-three master's programmes and one professional doctorate which are accredited by the BPS. It was also in the 1970s that the focus of research began cycling back round to wellbeing. The focus had shifted to mental more than physical wellbeing through looking at stress in the workplace, and active wellness not just the absence of injuries. This is something explored further in Chapter 4. Recruitment and selection remained and remains a major area of research and practical application. Again, the focus has shifted. Early research focused on getting the right man (and it was man) for the job at that moment in time. Research has now shifted to look at selection more broadly: would some people be better at a given job after a short amount of training (aptitude, rather than current ability); how does diversity in the workplace benefit; is the job defined in the best way possible right now or can work tasks be split up differently. At the same time the practicalities of selection have changed. It is now mostly online: big data means that there are more opportunities to compare aspects of individuals, and even selection processes have changed with the increasing use of games-based recruitment. These issues are explored in the next chapter. Leadership became an increasing focus of research, and some fields which had been very important early on in the profession's history began to become discrete professions of their own. What was initially an exploration of human–machine interaction and a major feature of the BPS curriculum has gradually become a separate profession of ergonomist though aspects of this work are still performed by occupational psychologists, and some individuals have dual accreditations. Whilst health psychology is already a discrete profession, there is also a more gradual shift of some aspects of health in the workplace to become separate with an increasing number of focused master's courses which look at the psychology of health in the workplace. It is an ever-evolving profession.

CURRENT POSITION

Work psychology is an academic area and a practice which is highly impacted by current political and social issues. Research often follows immediate concerns raised by society, and as a result a topic may be highly studied for years or decades before being almost completely ignored. Similarly, practising work psychologists will find that the projects and tasks they work on will reflect both new legislation in a country but also societal pressures. Therefore, it is important to consider what features of the modern workplace have current effects. It is common to read prosaicisms about how this current era involves more change than any other period. Such clichés ignore most of previous changes, downplaying their importance in the moment. It is worth remembering that whilst the 21st century may seem fast paced, the 20th century took us from horse and cart to space travel, from quill and ink to supercomputers and from women being chattel to almost universal sufferage through two world wars and massive global migration. Similarly the 19th century moved people from slavery to emancipation, through the collapse of five major world empires, though industrial revolutions and mass urbanisation. Every time is eventful if you are living through it. The changing features of modern societies and workplaces we should reflect on split into two: those which reflect continuing change and those which are novel to this time.

Discussion regarding political and social issues which are having an ongoing impact on the world of work are often focused on negative features or negative aspects of the change. An example is the changing type of work with increased automation and job specialisation. This is gradually leading to the removal of both low- and high-end jobs whilst having little impact on those in the middle. The negative position is that this leads to unemployment. However, this is only the case within specific economic systems. It can mean increased opportunities for current employees to engage in more meaningful and pleasurable work. Historically efficiencies have led societies as a whole (though notably not individuals necessarily) to be able to engage in more cultural activities, learning and creating. Increased diversity in the workforce with gradually achieved equality for historically disadvantaged groups for example women and those with disabilities is a positive change which can lead to new issues to explore for work psychologists such as how to organise work and the workplace. This work also needs to take account of the way in which organisations are changing anyway in response to pressure to cut costs resulting from increasing globalisation of markets. This is leading to changed organisational styles: increased outsourcing of functions (for example payroll, manufacturing or cleaning), delayering and downsizing. This can mean increased workloads for individual employees and reduced job security for individuals working through agencies or on contract work.

There are also a range of relatively new issues which impact current work psychology practices and research. Shockingly it is only within the last ten to fifteen years that work psychology has begun to consider work in developing countries, in part due to heightened societal awareness of the impacts of Western-based multinationals in these countries. Increased globalisation is slowly leading to a more global approach in work psychology too. The issue of the ageing work population, and dramatically reduced reproduction rate, is of immediate interest to work psychologists. Globally the average fertility rate has halved over the last fifty years. In highly developed countries this often equates to a negative reproduction rate. The effects of people living longer, having fewer children and needing longer care all impact work type and availability with increasing service and care roles and less opportunity for upward progression for the young as older workers retire at older ages. There are also changed working practices: increased remote working in many sectors and the growth of the gig economy and what is euphemistically known as the 'side hustle' meaning many people are precariously employed across multiple jobs, often far in excess of full-time hours.

These changes mean that work psychology is an ever-evolving discipline. The BPS last updated its curriculum for Stage 1 training (master's level) in 2017 with providers rolling out their new courses in 2018. The Stage 2 training (chartership) was last updated in 2020 reflecting changed priorities for Occupational Psychologists. This will be covered later in this chapter. The current Stage 1 curriculum includes five major knowledge areas, most UK master's use these five as the basis for their core modules. They align to five of the chapters of this book. These five are psychological assessment at work (Chapter 2); learning, training and development (Chapter 3); leadership, engagement and motivation (Chapter 6); wellbeing and work (Chapter 4); and work design, organisational change and development (Chapter 5). In addition to these content areas, master's courses must cover some cross-cutting themes which draw together key aspects of the way in which psychologists work and impact all areas of work. These include diversity, fairness, gender and cultural influences. Students are also taught about ethical practice, the science practitioner approach and research methods to facilitate ongoing research in practice settings as well as to support the dissertation component of the course which makes up a third of these programmes. Some examples of how this curriculum has advanced from previous iterations concern both content areas and research techniques taught. The previous curriculum had eight areas, rather than the current five. One area which has been reduced or subsumed under others is 'human–machine interaction.' Much of this work has become more specialised and undertaken by other professionals. In contrast, consumer psychology has been introduced into the BPS curriculum: something not previously covered. Over time the research methods taught have evolved. Early courses focused on more quantitative measures and positivist approaches whereas interpretivist approaches and qualitative techniques are now actively taught alongside cutting-edge techniques in areas such as neuroscience. An example is how the neuroscience technique fMRI is used to explore brain activity as consumers make decisions about products and how they think and feel about consumer products.

Moving forwards there are a number of hot topics in work psychology at the moment: areas which require both further research and practical interventions to apply the evidence already available. Firstly, there is what is termed humanitarian psychology. This is the work done to understand work in developing nations and focuses primarily on wellbeing and safety issues. Secondly there is still extensive work to do in relation to diversity of workforces. This theme has, to date, focused significantly on how to increase labour market participation of disadvantaged groups and how to ensure recruitment and selection is fair. Looking forwards the focus has shifted from simple diversity to the notion of inclusion. The difference is that diversity is about people being present within the workplace. Inclusion is about those people having power, autonomy and influence, being embedded at all levels, not just in entry roles with recognition of the specific knowledge brought by people from different backgrounds and experiences and how that is good for the whole organisation and whole society. A third issue is about how real people operate. Traditionally economic models have been applied to humans, yet research demonstrates that humans are not rational decision-makers, and such rational economic models are not helpful. They need to be replaced with understanding of the behavioural principles underlying human actions. An example is in how humans perceive risk level and likelihood: they are fundamentally optimistic. Using psychological principles, equipment and processes can be redesigned to accommodate systematic failures in human judgement. This applies at all levels from how senior decision-making is conducted to whether employees adhere to existing policies. This links to the fourth major topic of interest: how people actually use technologies. This area considers both safety and efficiencies in using technologies from machines to websites. It covers areas such as human cognitive load and perceptual limits whilst also considering how to evaluate usage, how it is actually done. A practical example which will likely resonate is thinking about how you produced a document and the 'tips' people have given you over the years for how to do so efficiently. Designers assumed users would use these from the start, but you have likely completed the same action inefficiently for years without ever finding out how to do it correctly. Much of this work is less superficial though and crosses over with aspects of culture change and the need to redesign the technology itself. This is particularly the case when it impacts safety. How technologies are used in and out of the workplace has become increasingly important in a post-Covid era where there is increasing distance working. An example of issues explored is how to generate 'telepresence', a sense of being in a working environment when you are not, and the need to stimulate social interaction between workers who are geographically separated, maybe in different timezones or from very different cultures. Finally, there has been an increasing interest in the notion of positive psychology in recent years: exploring what works and why it works. Topics of interest here include the notion of flow in the workplace (being so into your work you don't notice time passing); authentic leadership and its effects; and how the psychological capital of individuals can be enhanced.

WORKING PRACTICES

In the UK the term Occupational Psychologist is a protected title and can only be used by people who have achieved chartership with the British Psychological Society (BPS). It is common to then register with the Health and Care Professions Council (HCPC) as a Practitioner Psychologist, another protected title, but this is not compulsory. In order to qualify as an Occupational Psychologist, the Graduate Basis for Registration must first be obtained. Most commonly this is done by passing a BPS-approved psychology undergraduate degree. Trainees then need to complete both the Qualification in Occupational Psychology (QOP) Stage 1 and Stage 2. Usually Stage 1 is completed in the form of a BPS-approved master's degree and Stage 2 as an in-work doctoral level of study conducted under the guidance of a Practitioner Psychologist. More recently higher education providers have begun exploring providing a combined Stage 1 and Stage 2 qualification, but as of 2023 there isn't one yet available. Many students complete only the part one of the QOP and then go on to work in similar roles but using non-protected titles such as business psychologist. In North America, Australia and much of Europe the expectation is that psychologists working in this area will have completed either a research degree in psychology, gaining a PhD, or a practitioner doctorate, gaining a PsyD. However, it is still also possible to work in the area, having only completed a master's degree as well. The names used for these differ, however, and they are more commonly called industrial or organisational psychology. A less common route is to complete a master's in business administration (MBA).

Occupational Psychologists work in all sectors of the economy though they may have many different titles. The key principle which ties all of the roles together is that Occupational Psychologists use scientific methods and psychological principles to make workplaces more efficient, more diverse, more fair, safer and nicer places to be. This might be by helping individuals develop and be ready for the workplace through career counselling, training, etc. It might also be by changing business practices and environments to suit people better, for example through better selection processes, wellbeing intervention, or redesign of physical spaces, policies, practices or jobs. Critically psychologists will use the consultancy cycle in their work. This involves contracting, information gathering and analysis of the problem, formulating an evidence-based plan, implementing and reviewing plans and finally evaluating. Evaluation may involve both quantitative and qualitative measures and will consider how different levels of an organisation have been impacted, from the individual employees, or stakeholders, to groups within the organisation, or the whole organisation. It will also consider factors such as whether organisational culture has been impacted. Occupational psychologists are involved in both explaining behaviours within an organisation (problem analysis) as well as providing solutions to increase efficiency and wellbeing. Some will work in research roles both in higher education and in private research organisations. Others work on a self-employed basis as consultants or coaches. Occupational Psychologists also work in the civil service, in the UK big employers are the Department for Work and Pensions, the police force, and the defence sector. Within private firms Occupational Psychologists work both for large organisations in a specific team, or as part of the human resources department, as well as in smaller psychology consultancies, who are hired by other organisations.

WORKING IN THE PUBLIC SECTOR ACROSS ENGLAND, SCOTLAND AND WALES: CASE STUDY

The Department for Work and Pensions' Work Psychology Service is one of the leading employers of Occupational Psychologists across England, Scotland and Wales. Our regional teams of psychologists provide two core, specialist services – both strictly underpinned by our profession's standards and regulatory requirements. Our work is derived from best available evidence, conducted in accordance with ethical, legal and reflective practice standards, and our interventions are structured through the consultancy cycle.

First, we provide a specialist service to individuals in receipt of welfare benefits that wish to secure our support to progress into and sustain employment. It's a role where occupational psychology has a direct, positive impact upon the lives of citizens, given our work is to support those who are socially excluded, vulnerable or otherwise disadvantaged when it comes to employment opportunities. As psychologists, we use our specialist knowledge, skills (e.g., coaching techniques) and resources (e.g., psychometric tests, work samples) to identify an individual's strengths for employment – whilst factoring in health and disability circumstances – to maximise the fit between an individual and the work they might wish do. The aim: that they can flourish in employment. Our delivery methods can include one-to-one assessments, case conferences and group-based events. We also directly support employers on how to facilitate this within their workplace.

Second, we design, deliver and evaluate training programmes to help thousands of colleagues acquire knowledge and practise job-relevant skills that can improve customer outcomes (e.g., training for interviewing and coaching skills). This makes the role varied, and rewarding.

Daniel Sharples, Principal Occupational Psychologist with the Department for Work and Pensions

WORKING IN THE PUBLIC SECTOR IN NORTHERN IRELAND: ADVICE

If you are considering a career in occupational psychology, there are two personal qualities valuable for career success and satisfaction: Firstly, curiosity: as an OP you are working with organisations, teams and individuals, to diagnose and solve problems; having a natural curiosity will help keep you motivated and engaged. Secondly, a love of learning: when working as an OP you will need to continuously improve and maintain your knowledge and skills; enjoying learning will help you stay on top of the latest research

As a Trainee OP in the Northern Ireland Civil Service, I work in a small team supporting public sector service delivery. I am an internal consultant and operate across the five areas of occupational psychology. This role is exciting and dynamic, providing opportunities to work with a range of stakeholders on activities including: conducting assessments to support those with health conditions seeking or retaining employment; supporting leaders in their own professional development and in their capacity of supporting their teams; and delivering training and coaching interventions to support workplace wellbeing. What I like most about my job is the positive and measurable impact that I can have on people's lives in the workplace and beyond.

Bronagh Mahon, Higher Occupational Psychologist, Department for Communities, Northern Ireland

SUMMARY

In summary, we can say that work psychology has been an important influence on workplaces, practices and processes over the last hundred years. Psychologists have provided advice to organisations and built systems which make workplaces more diverse, more fair, safer and more pleasant places to be. However, the world of work is continuously evolving, and psychologists are now turning to new challenges such as the move towards working at a distance, increased globalisation including globally located team members, generational shifts in attitudes towards work, the availability of big data and social media amongst others. National-level lockdowns as Covid precautions led to major shifts in how people feel about work, as well as developments in technologies, and have as yet to be fully explored by research on how this impacts effective workplace interventions.

Now we have explored what work psychology involves, where it came from and how to become a psychologist, the following chapters will look at the five main areas of occupational psychology which include: psychological assessment at work; learning, training and development; wellbeing at work; work design, organisational change and development; and leadership, engagement and motivation before finishing with a specific look at research and practice in work psychology and the future of work psychology.

RECOMMENDATIONS FOR FURTHER READING

British Psychological Society (2020). Division of Occupational Psychology. Available at: www.bps.org.uk/member-microsites/division-occupational-psychology (accessed: 18 June 2022).

Picard, D. (2018). *Analyzing the Human Factor in British Industrial Psychology, 1919–1939.* PhD thesis, Vanderbilt University. Available at: https://ir.vanderbilt.edu/handle/1803/15465?show=full (accessed: 18 June 2022).

Shimmin, S., and Wallis, D. (1994). *Fifty Years of Occupational Psychology in Britain.* Leicester: British Psychological Society.

PSYCHOLOGICAL
ASSESSMENT AT WORK

This chapter covers perhaps the most common area of occupational psychology and that which is also most often undertaken by non-psychologists. There is no definitive record of destinations of occupational psychology graduates (British Psychological Society, 2012). However, it is clear that selection and assessment proves a common first job. This can be working in a consultancy specifically focusing on designing and delivering psychological assessments, in a bespoke psychometric consultancy, or it can be working within a larger organisation, typically in the human resources department. Because all organisations need to recruit, there is a large demand for staff to work in this field, and there are significant overlaps with other job roles. In a large organisation you might also find yourself working alongside other staff such as recruitment consultants or human resources officers.

This chapter considers how to use psychological tools and theory to recruit the 'ideal candidate'. Firstly, we explore what the concept of ideal candidate means before defining the criteria we should use during the selection process. Next the practical steps of the recruitment and selection cycle will be described with a particular focus on how to evaluate whether this is an effective process. Finally, we will consider some more innovative methods being used and then current issues in

DOI: 10.4324/9781315169880-2

this sector. Throughout the chapter short case study examples will illustrate selection and assessment in practice.

Defining the best person for a job involves more than effective selection techniques. The very best selection tools are only correlated at 0.65 with job performance (Schmidt and Hunter, 1998). This is because job performance concerns more than ability. It is determined by motivation, environmental factors, leadership style and colleagues' performance, amongst other variables. Therefore the 'ideal candidate' should be thought about more widely than just who performs best on selection tests. It is outside the scope of this chapter to explore this point in depth. However, an example should illustrate the point. A Spanish organisation has an average employee age of 54, with most employees retiring at 65. It is predicted 30% of staff will retire in the next five years. Their greater experience means older applicants are more likely to outperform younger applicants using ability tests. However, the organisation needs to lower the average age. Age discrimination is illegal throughout the EU, so they can't deliberately hire younger people. As we progress through the chapter bear this example in mind and think about how the organisation might deal with this conundrum, considering what would make a candidate 'ideal'.

CORE CRITERIA

Imagine being asked how best to move a series of barrels up a mountain when applying for a childcare position, or for your date of birth to evaluate the alignments of planets at your birth to see if you should be accepted onto a training course, a sample of handwriting to assess your personality, or for someone who has hired you in the past to comment on your suitability for another job. All of these four techniques have been/are used in selecting candidates, yet only two are able to predict future performance accurately; and despite that only one should be used. In deciding which are appropriate there are some core criteria which should be applied. These are: validity, reliability, legality, practicality, candidate acceptance and ethics. We will look at these in turn to see what they mean in practice and how they should be considered.

CORE CRITERIA

* ★ Validity
* ★ Reliability
* ★ Legality
* ★ Practicality
* ★ Candidate acceptance
* ★ Ethics

Validity is arguably the most important of these criteria. Validity refers broadly to whether something measures what it claims to be measuring. In psychology we think about both concurrent and predictive validity. Concurrent validity, in this context, means that a measurement in one domain correlates with performance in another. For example, payment of a bonus may be directly related to performance selling cars. Equally, persuasive ability of a salesperson may be directly related to their ability to sell cars. Predictive validity is concerned with whether measuring a trait at this point in time can be linked to future performance. We turn to look at our first example here: moving barrels up a hill. Initially this may not seem to relate to childcare skill, but this measure can have predictive validity. This task was used by the British Civil Service to tap into an individual's problem-solving ability. Problem-solving skill was independently assessed to be important to a childcare role. Consequently performance on such a problem-solving task could be linked to later performance as a childcare worker. The selection measure had predictive validity.

After validity, reliability is the next most commonly considered criterion for assessing the benefits of a selection tool. Reliability is concerned with whether the outcome is consistent: if the same tool was used in the same conditions with the same people would the same results be gained. An example of a measure with high reliability would be using horoscopes. If one believed that planetary alignment at birth impacted future traits or performance then the same data would be used each time to assess the candidate and the same outcome would result. Hopefully, this example illustrates that reliability alone is not sufficient. It is only important when considered in conjunction with validity. The measure used must also be valid: i.e. a true measure of what it aims to assess.

Having a measure which is valid and reliable implies that it must also be legal, and the example given here is somewhat tongue in cheek. However, validity and reliability can be present in a measure which is not legal to use. Again, to illustrate the point an extreme case will be given. Almost every legal system places a duty of care on employers to ensure the safety of their service users, customers and staff. This legislation could stop a valid and reliable assessment being used. If we were to select the best surgeon, taxi driver or pilot, we could, as part of our selection process, ask them to engage in surgery, driving or flight. This would fairly test their abilities in comparison to each other allowing appropriate discrimination between the applicants. However, this would not be safe and so not legal. However, a low stakes trial could be valid, reliable and legal, for example asking a checkout operative to check out real groceries, or a stenographer to take real notes.

It might be possible to think of alternatives in the last scenario which would make the process legal. For example, the pilot could showcase their skills using a simulation. The surgeon could be asked to demonstrate 'operating' on a piece of meat. If creating a simulation of the real work like this it is important that it has fidelity, i.e. it accurately reflects the real situation. In this example the taxi driver wouldn't have fidelity in the simulation if there weren't noise, smells and other stimuli in their simulation vehicle. The surgeon wouldn't have fidelity if she were asked to 'operate' on a plastic dummy rather than a piece of meat which feels, smells and moves differently. The issue with creating selection methods with high fidelity is that they can be expensive. Expense is one of the elements to be considered in relation to the fourth criterion we use: practicality. Practicality dictates whether a measure can be used at all. The practicality criterion is broader than just expense. It considers whether the desired selection test can be completed in the available environment and with the available resources. For example, we might want to assess a teacher's skills by watching them teach but might not have a classroom/computer/projector/audience available to allow that. Practicality also encompasses other parameters, e.g. whether there is time to undertake this measure. It also links to our fifth criterion: candidate acceptance.

Candidate acceptance considers whether the person applying for the role is motivated to conduct the tests being asked of them. There are two main reasons why they might not be. Firstly, they may think the demands are too great. For example, asking people to undertake a week's assessment of their skills as a machinist would accurately gauge their skill. However, it is unlikely they would be willing to give up that time. In this way candidate acceptance can be subsumed under the practicality criterion. However, there is also a second aspect which means, when designing assessments, it should be independently considered. This is because the test designer knows more about the test purpose than the person being assessed. We return to the earlier assessment: how best to move a series of barrels up a mountain. This was one of many scenarios given in the UK Civil Service to assess a range of applicants, including those applying for a childcare position. The selection test was initially designed for use with military personnel, and for them it made sense: how could they move resources in difficult terrain. However, the test isn't to assess knowledge of this particular problem, rather it is to assess problem-solving approaches and skills. Therefore, whilst it doesn't initially look to be a valid measure of the childcare role, it is valid. The employer also knows it is reliable as a measure because they have used it extensively and analysed the data over time. It fulfils the requirements to be legal and practical (it is given as a spoken scenario rather than an actual test). However, lack of candidate acceptance of it may impact their motivation to respond and may link to later propensity to make claims of unfair treatment (see Terpstra et al., 1999, and Williams et al., 2013). For many organisations applicants are also customers too, and so it is important that each person leaves the process feeling they have been fairly treated.

The final criterion we need to consider is: would the test be ethical? We have already explored some assessments here which wouldn't be ethical but are already ruled out because, for example, they are not legal. However, ethics needs to be considered on its own as well, in particular when a test does discriminate appropriately but we don't know why. To explore this idea we return to one of the first assessments we described: using your date of birth to evaluate the alignments of planets at your birth to see if you should be accepted onto a training course. Surprisingly this might pass all of the other tests. There is nothing legally to prevent you using this measure. Candidates might accept it depending on their culture and own beliefs about horoscopes. It is cheap and quick to do, therefore it is practical. It is also reliable because your date of birth doesn't change and so if the same rules were applied for interpreting that date then you would have 100% reliability over time and if the measure was done by somebody different. Initially what may seem surprising is that it may also be valid, but when we explore the reasons why it is valid we see it is not ethical. Remember that validity is a measure of whether the test assesses what it claims to measure: in this case whether your star sign impacts performance on an apprenticeship. People whose star sign is Libra are significantly more likely to perform well in a first job or training than a Leo. The reason is not because of their star sign per se though. It is because of their age. Libras went to school when they were nearly five in comparison to Leos who had just turned four. This 11-month advantage leads to better outcomes throughout schooling (Dhuey et al., 2017). Understanding this advantage shows us it is not ethical to use a mechanism which rewards individuals because of this chance of birth.

So now we have outlined the key criteria we need to use we turn to look at the different stages in the selection cycle we need to consider. In each we should keep in mind: validity, reliability, legality, practicality, candidate acceptance and ethics as each decision is made.

CASE STUDY EXAMPLE: BLIND HIRING

The security and stability of jobs in South Korea's civil service make it a desirable employer for young Koreans. Consequently, there are large numbers of applicants. Until recently applying for these jobs involved giving intrusive details such as family background and blood type as well as other details which are neither valid nor ethical in looking at performance. In 2017 the government introduced new selection processes: removing the requirement to include photographs and other non-work-related details, bringing it in line with most developed countries where such questions are illegal. South Korea went further by removing other identifying details linked to unconscious bias such as schools attended. The main selection tool used currently is a biannual selection exam, common across all different roles from firefighters to accountants.

RECRUITMENT AND SELECTION CYCLE

Work psychologists talk about recruitment and selection as a cycle. By this they mean feedback from each new employee is used to assess how effective the previous selection process was and allow modification for the next round of recruitment. This section looks at the stages of the cycle and how they interdepend.

When an organisation identifies a vacancy the first step is to establish what that role involves and therefore what are the features of the ideal candidate. Here the term job analysis is used as a catch-all but this process is also described as task analysis, role analysis, competency analysis, competency modelling and defining job requirements. There is a lack of consensus among experts' definitions of the process (Schippmann et al., 2000), but essentially job analysis involves defining what the component job parts are, and what a person must be able to do to perform that job successfully.

Job analysis focuses either on the work involved (task analysis) or on the characteristics of the typical or best current role incumbent (worker-oriented job analysis). Task analysis is effective if there is one definitive way to best perform the job, for example sewing clothes together. An example of a task analysis approach is observation: people currently in the role are observed in their day-to-day performance to see what tasks they do, for how long and in collaboration with whom. It does not accommodate well jobs which can be performed in different ways. For example, selling a car can be done either by being tenacious and pushing a customer hard to buy on this one occasion or by being seemingly laid back and building a relationship to sell the same customer a new car every three years. Either way works but they lead to quite different job descriptions being produced.

Worker-oriented job analysis is better for drawing out what knowledge, skills and abilities (KSAs) would be required of someone in that role and can be particularly helpful for establishing threshold and differentiating competencies. Threshold competencies are those required to perform effectively in the role. Differentiating competencies are those which represent superior performance. Most worker-oriented job analysis involves interviewing role incumbents. The Position Analysis Questionnaire (PAQ) is a standardised way of conducting these interviews. Ratings are given for 195 potential KSAs which might be required in this role, and the interviewer completes it after discussing with the job incumbent and then produces a person speci-fication from the outputs. This specification may incorporate more information than that gathered from the job analysis though. Here we need to think again about our 'ideal candidate'. In Spain, for example, social intelligence and interpersonal insight are regarded as particu-larly important in selection because of the high value placed on team fit in that culture. So, if the individual was working in that environ-ment these KSAs may be added on to all job descriptions and person specifications regardless of role. Ultimately, if budget allows, a multi-method approach to job analysis is best, and a psychologist would look for convergence of methods.

The next step in the cycle is choosing the method(s) which best discriminate between applicants. This must be done before attract-ing applicants because selection may start at the application stage. For example, Marks and Spencer's graduate training scheme requires applicants to successfully complete a personality psychometric test in order to access the application form. Similarly, the British Civil Service incorporates a range of ability tests as part of what is termed the initial sift. Sometimes recruiters need to reduce the number of applicants to a tenth or less as part of this sift, and so it is important the tools used conform to the criteria discussed earlier, i.e. they are valid, reliable, legal, practical and ethical and that candidates accept them as such.

An important decision to be made is whether a funnel or summa-tive model is to be used. A funnel model gradually removes appli-cants during a series of assessments until the ideal candidate(s) remains. This method is most effective when only threshold performance is of interest, for example when there are many roles to fill and not many applicants. Most call centres recruit in this way: most applicants are hired and they are only removed from the process if they can't meet the threshold level of performance required in each task. A summative model operates differently. In this approach all applicants take part in all assessments and are awarded a score for performance in each. The cumulative score is then compared and the ideal candidate chosen on the basis of that. This approach is better if a job can be redesigned to mitigate a weakness in an otherwise good candidate. For example, it is desirable if a product designer can also persuade potential customers of the product's value but not essential. If they perform well on all other assessments but poorly on persuasion, one would still prefer to hire this applicant in contrast to an applicant who scored medium across all assessments and remove this element of the role. In practice most selection processes incorporate elements of each method at different stages: funnel early on and summative later.

Traditional methods which are used to assess candidates include interviews, analysis of biographical data (bio data) and psychometric tests. Interviews are very popular and are used by most organisations. Huffcutt and Arthur (1994) classify interviews on a four-point scale on the basis of their structure and demonstrate interview validity varies dramatically in relation to structure: the more structured the better. Structure refers to the extent to which questions asked of different applicants are the same and how pre-defined the analysis of interviewees' responses is. Bio data incorporates hard facts, e.g. whether an applicant has a specific qualification, and what is termed soft bio data. Soft bio data refers to more abstract information which needs to be interpreted, e.g. the level of perseverance a person shows. Bio data is primarily gathered from CVs/résumés/application forms so the applicant constructs it themselves. For this reason soft bio data use is more contentious, being less reliable. Psychometric assessments are another widely used selection technique. The most common form of psychometric assessments used in selection assess in order: ability, personality and values. In all domains genuine psychometric measures can only be used by people who hold the appropriate accreditations. In the UK the main accreditations are governed by the British Psychological Society, and further information can be found at https://ptc.bps.org.uk/ for those interested in being licensed in their use.

Once selection processes have been decided attempts should be made to attract appropriate candidates. At this stage it is important to consider both the content of advertisements and their placement. If operating in an area where positive discrimination is not permitted one might aim to disproportionately attract applicants from under-represented groups. Considering the earlier example: an organisation wanting to attract more applicants who are younger should consider how these individuals are most likely to job search. It is not a requirement to advertise a job. Indeed it is estimated 70% of jobs are never formally advertised. If a job is advertised, though, most countries legally require that it is fairly advertised. An extreme example illustrates this point: it would be indirect discrimination to advertise a job only via posters in men's changing rooms. It would, however, be legal to place an advertisement in a magazine predominantly read by females, if females were underrepresented in this role and assuming other adverts existed appealing to the full range of potential applicants. Attracting candidates incorporates more than placement though. The advertisement itself needs to be appealing to the target group. This might mean drawing out specific aspects of the role, e.g., if the working hours are flexible this may appeal disproportionately to women who are more likely to be responsible for childcare. Images used are also important, for example, if younger applicants are desired then showing them in the images used can help.

Once applications have been made assessors need to be trained and the assessments completed and scored. Assessor training is, unfortunately, rarely performed, impacting both validity and reliability of assessments. Chapman and Zweig (2005) found typically 34% of interviewers had received formal training in this task. Lack of training is correlated with increased assessor bias. Assessor bias is a major issue in selection and can result from conscious discrimination as well as unconscious biases. Chunking is a solution recommended by the Behavioural Insights Team, a company established by the UK government to apply behavioural science to policy. They have developed a tool called Applied which asks applicants questions specific to the role they've applied for. These answers are then anonymised, collated (chunked) and sent to existing organisational staff to be rated. In this way the impact of any assessor biases are reduced for each candidate.

Unfair advantages can result from candidate as well as assessor behaviour. Two major forms are explored. Firstly, candidates may 'fake good'. This term describes candidates recognising the traits or attitudes desirous to the organisation and presenting themselves, inaccurately, as having these traits. Donovan and Dwight (2014) found in their study of applicants who were subsequently hired about half faked on at least one dimension of a self-report measure. This behaviour impacted the validity of the measures because the applicants who faked good were significantly lower performing than non-fakers based on performance data collected five months after initial training. Secondly, candidates may deliberately cheat in the selection process. This is a particular danger when part of the assessment is conducted remotely. Candidates may seek help in responding to assessments, ask another person to complete tests for them or otherwise cheat. It is vital then that where decisions are made based on remote assessments that tests are replicated, face to face, for candidates who have reached these later stages of the process. Despite the need to replicate, remote assessment is still cost effective. This is because it is used to remove a large volume of potential applicants. Theoretically it should not remove any who should have remained in the pool (false negatives), but it does keep in some who should have been removed (false positives). These false positives are then removed when the assessment is replicated later in the process.

CASE STUDY EXAMPLE: ASSESSMENT IN PRACTICE AT A LARGE ORGANISATION

The core criteria that should be met when selecting candidates apply to large organisations as they do to smaller ones. However, large organisations must overcome additional challenges to ensure their assessment practices meet these criteria.

One of the key issues for large organisations is the high volume of positions they need to fill and the corresponding applications that they receive for those roles. If we consider that an organisation of over 10,000 employees has an employee turnover rate of 15% a year, then that company will need to fill a minimum of 1,500 jobs a year assuming they replace each person that has left. Assuming that an employer receives around 40 applications per role, then the company would need to sift through 60,000 applications. This figure is likely to be even higher for companies recruiting people in line with growth. Therefore, there is an even greater need for a selection process to meet the criteria of practicality. As an example, reviewing a CV for relevant skills and experience is a selection method that is commonly accepted to meet all the above criteria. However, if this were to be the first stage of a selection process for a large company, it may not be practical to review such a large number of applications. This is particularly important considering that recruitment is often managed within a single department of an organisation, such as HR.

To overcome this initial challenge, large organisations often include methods of assessment at the start of their selection processes that are time- and resource-effective ways of reducing the volume of applications, and which can predict performance in across a large amount of job roles. A construct that is commonly assessed in this case is cognitive ability, as research has shown this is a construct that predicts workplace performance, even more so in cognitively demanding roles (Schmidt and Hunter, 1998). This also ensures that the methods of assessment used in the selection process also meet the criteria outlined so far.

Given the challenges mentioned thus far that large organisations often face, particularly in relation to volume, large organisations often implement and are reliant on technology to support their assessment practice. Applicant tracking systems (ATSs) are one such example, which provide a database for a company's recruitment efforts and which can automate a great deal of HR processes, such as the administration of online assessments or recorded video interviews.

Once applicants have been narrowed down to a more manageable volume, there is a need to assess other areas that will help identify the best candidate. One challenge that this presents for large organisations is how to enable hiring managers in a business, outside the recruitment team, to assess these areas and make their own hiring decisions, whilst also ensuring decisions are made fairly, consistently and legally within the business. This relates to the criteria not only of reliability but also of legality, candidate acceptance and ethics. Taking the example of an interview, one way a large organisation can achieve this is by providing interview guides and scoring sheets for interviewers to use. This allows interviewers to ask their own job specific questions while also evaluating candidates consistently using more objective scoring. Large organisations also implement other resources to support their assessment practices, for example training on effective interviewing and assessing, as well as other topics related to decision-making such as unconscious bias training.

EVALUATION AND RETURN ON INVESTMENT

Evaluation is an intrinsic part of the recruitment cycle, but it is considered separately here to emphasise its significance. Despite evaluation being critical to assess the validity of the measures which have been used in that specific context, unfortunately, it is still often neglected, and organisations might use the same assessment tools repeatedly without evaluating whether they are appropriate for recruitment to this organisation. One of the reasons for this is that the immediate benefits of evaluation are necessarily clear. Psychologists typically refer to return on investment (ROI) as a concept to encourage organisations to complete this element. Processes for calculating ROI are discussed after a consideration of the legal and ethical impetus to evaluate.

Without conscious awareness it is possible to design a recruitment process which discriminates unfairly against a particular group of applicants. Ongoing evaluation ensures this is recognised and changed as soon as possible. Failure to do so can leave the organisation open to legal challenge. Evaluation involves quantitative and qualitative checking. At each selection stage quantitative checks should be undertaken to assess whether a particular group has been disproportionately unsuccessful. If there are discrepancies, for example on the basis of gender, age or race then a qualitative assessment needs to be made to assess what features of that assessment might be impacting. For example, a manufacturing organisation identifies that whilst lots of young people apply for a role only 10% pass the initial assessment in comparison to 80% of older applicants. A qualitative investigation of the assessment shows that it comprises an interview in which the questions are focused on experience rather than ability: candidates are asked about whether they have constructed goods in the past rather than whether they are able to do so in the future. As a consequence, younger applicants are being removed from the process as false negatives and potentially have a legal case against the employer for indirect age discrimination. Ongoing evaluation also involves checking on the scoring of particular assessors and calibrating the ratings they give applicants. Failure to do so could lead to lack of reliability in the process.

In addition to this ongoing evaluation a formal evaluation with ROI should be conducted after the jobs have been filled. It is important to leave sufficient time after the new employees have started so that they are performing at their typical level before doing this though. In an ideal scenario data would be available about the performance of all role applicants. This could then be compared against how they performed in the assessment process and the degree of correlation could be calculated. Evaluation is always slightly imperfect though as the data is only available from successful candidates. A variety of data can be used to undertake this assessment but typically this includes both quantitative measures of performance, e.g. number of items sold, or units made, as well as qualitative measures such as supervisor's ratings or customer feedback. It is worth remembering that the correlation between on-the-job performance and performance in the selection exercises will never be 100% because other factors impact on the job performance such as motivation and interactions with colleagues.

Once other evaluations are complete a formal ROI calculation can be completed. There are two main ways of calculating ROI. Either the selection process can be evaluated by looking at the difference in performance between the applicants chosen (the Brogden–Hunter method) or efficacy of the system can be established by seeing if the selection process ruled out any false positives, i.e. people who are unable to do the role effectively (the Taylor–Russell method). The former process is most useful for roles where there are many applicants, the latter is best when there are not many more applicants than jobs available and recruiters can be less picky about who to employ. The calculations for Brogden–Hunter are complex and outside the remit of a book of this depth. An example of the Taylor–Russell method is presented below.

WORKED EXAMPLE: ROI ON A SELECTION PROCESS

The Taylor–Russell method is used when there is no variation in performance that affects success. An example might be a firefighter. Each firefighter either can or cannot fight fires. To work out ROI of the system used firstly the validity of the system needs to be established, i.e. what proportion of people recruited using this system weren't able to do the job. In the original selection process an interview was used with 0.4 validity. In the new process a work sample is undertaken with a validity of 0.6. It is expensive though as the work sample costs £50 per applicant to run.

We also need to know the difficulty of the job calculated as the percentage of people who would be satisfactory if we selected at random and how many people applied for the role. We estimate the difficulty in this case as 50%, i.e. picked at random half of people could do the role. We select one in five of the people who apply for this role. With this basic information, i.e. validity of measure, selection ratio, difficulty of job, we can work out ROI using the tables produced by Lawshe et al. (1958).

Difficulty of the job is used in selecting the correct table. From the appropriate table we can see that the original method with 0.4 validity and a 20% selection ratio means 51% of recruits can do the job. Our new method with 0.6 validity leads to 64% of successful applicants being able to do the job. It costs £10,000 to train one person who subsequently fails so the new method leads to £360,000 in wasted training costs compared to £490,000 in the old method. We also have to account for the assessment costs though. In this hypothetical recruitment of firefighters we tested five times as many applicants as the hundred we finally recruited so that cost £25,000. So overall the ROI of our new more efficient method was £105,000, or £1,050 per firefighter recruited.

OTHER SELECTION METHODS

So far we have considered traditional selection processes, but this is a dynamic field with innovations particularly for those organisations who do volume recruitment, e.g. National Health Service, Civil Service, supermarket chains and consultancies. These larger recruiters are more likely to consider validity as a primary criterion in designing their processes and recognise that it is important to consider ROI of methods, not just absolute costs. Consequently they are more likely to invest in methods which have higher upfront costs. One such example is short- or medium-term work trials. Some of the benefits of these are that they give both parties a realistic impression. They can be onerous for applicants though and are only really suitable if recruiting from pools who are not already in work. Some organisations use internships or work placements as a surreptitious work sample test: offering work to some participants. This is a highly contentious area as, it is argued, only those from affluent families are able to take part in such extended placements for little or no money, and organisations such as the National Union of Students in the UK and pressure group Pay Our Interns in the USA campaign against this practice as unethical and potentially illegal in nations with minimum wage legislation.

Some of the benefits of work placements can be extracted in a less contentious process: situational judgement tests. These tests can either be bought off the shelf, or to increase candidate acceptance and validity can be custom made by each organisation. Ideally they should be constructed using scenarios found during the job analysis phase. Each one should represent a real situation or issue in the job and applicants can be either given pre-set answers to choose from, or in more valid tests, give free text responses which are coded by the assessor according to pre-established answers. They are typically delivered respectively as written tests or as a structured interview.

Another form of interviewing is also gaining popularity and acceptance. Strengths-based recruitment is a standard practice in some area. For example, in Japan people are usually hired to a team not to a specific position. They are then assigned tasks according to their strengths and abilities. This idea is becoming more popular in the West recently. In this model of recruitment it makes sense to focus on what people can do well, and proponents of this approach argue that it leads to higher job performance. This is because people placed into roles based on their strengths are likely to be more motivated in those roles. Strengths-based approaches also tie in with another more recent development: the use of video résumés. CVs/résumés differ from application forms because they are less structured, allowing the applicant to foreground their strengths. They make it harder to compare candidates. Video résumés are growing in popularity as they are perceived by recruiters as being an effective way of assessing communication skills at the same time as showcasing the strengths the applicant wants to present. Thinking back to the criteria we use to assess selection methods, though, video résumés raise a couple of red flags. Firstly, candidates may be unwilling to be videoed, and so they can have low candidate acceptance. We might also question the ethics of the method because they allow recruiters to discriminate consciously or unconsciously on facets of the person which don't relate to the role. Aspects such as height, attractiveness and extent to which the individual's image conforms to traditional masculine and feminine facial structure have been shown in other arena to be forms of discrimination. Video résumés allow this to occur and so may also be illegal where there is discrimination legislation based on age, gender or transsexuality. As yet there have been no legal test cases about this however. These problems may be mitigated by using technology though.

Technology has been employed in the case of video interviews in recent years. These differ somewhat from video résumés because in this method the applicant has to respond to pre-set questions and therefore there is structure in the process and applicants can be compared more easily. Whilst these can be manually assessed, the rise of video interviews results from them being capable of being automated. Artificial intelligence can be used to score by looking for examples of: key words being used, an enthusiastic tone and body movement. This increased automation has two main benefits. Firstly, more candidates can be assessed cheaply. This means there is less likelihood of the false negative, i.e. losing a candidate who would be able to perform well, as part of an arbitrary first sift. Previously such first sifts would be against criteria such as exam performance in volume recruitment. The second benefit is that automated personalised feedback can be generated. This is likely to make the system more acceptable to the candidate and is more ethical given the amount of time applicants can give to applying for roles. The most dramatic innovation in selection in recent years is the development of interactive psychometrics using gaming technology. Psychometric testing has grown in popularity in the last twenty years with organisations recognising that this method's enhanced validity and reliability also make their selection processes more legally defensible. The recent movement towards gamification of these psychometrics means that the process becomes more valid as the tests tap into less obvious measures and assess skills in real time. However, it is important psychologists remain mindful of the need to retain candidate acceptance. If applicants perceive they have simply been asked to play games, they may be vocal about this and damage the organisation's reputation, and social media make it easy to get the message of a disgruntled applicant to a wide audience. Gamification takes various forms in these new psychometrics. At one level it means using features of game playing such as having scores, applicant moving through levels and unlocking rewards as well as having visible competition. At the other end of the spectrum it employs actual game-based assessments. Interested readers may want to look at organisations such as Arctic Shores and Pymetrics who create these types of assessments.

CURRENT ISSUES IN THE SECTOR

Selection and assessment is a dynamic area of research for psychology, and research is undertaken both by psychology academics as well as practitioners in the field. So people thinking about entering this specific sub-branch of the discipline are likely to be involved in some research, particularly if joining a consultancy. In this section some current issues are outlined in relation to giving feedback, the use of social media, the need to future focus, assessing maximal versus average performance, and traits which are desirable but hard to measure.

Candidates would like to receive feedback but in volume recruitment there may be thousands of applicants. Over time, organisations become more skilled at specifically targeting the individuals they want. However, at the early stages this can still mean numbers to assess are several orders of magnitude beyond those they eventually want to hire. Each applicant puts time and effort into that application and so would like feedback even if unsuccessful. This is both an ethical and a business issue as candidates may give negative publicity if they are unhappy with the process and indeed may be customers of the organisation themselves. Automation, as discussed earlier is going some of the way towards solving this dilemma, but it remains an area of discussion and debate in the field.

Technology may raise issues as well as solve them. The rise of social media usage raises questions about whether this should form part of the selection process. The multitude of horror stories about candidates losing jobs at the eleventh hour due to inappropriate posts demonstrates that employers, particularly smaller organisations, commonly undertake at least a superficial background check in this way. Landers and Schmidt (2016) draw out the main issues with social media as a data source. Firstly, individuals are presenting particular versions of themselves online which may not correlate with the candidates' on-the-job performance, and the way they can be seen online can be contaminated by the postings of others. This impacts the validity of what is seen. Despite this some researchers have attempted to use algorithms to develop predictive models of behaviour based on postings. These have so far not proven statistically valid in measuring personality though, which has been the research's main focus. Secondly, it may not be legal to conduct such searches as it can reveal irrelevant information about the individual such as race or religion which is not a legally defensible position. Thirdly, such searches are unlikely to be acceptable to candidates who could view them as invasions of privacy. This raises the issue of whether the practice is ethical at all. Indeed it can be argued that employers should not be concerned with out-of-work behaviours. Finally, it is not clear how, even if these issues were surmounted, an organisation could procedurally use this data. Currently there are no large organisations systematically incorporating this information, but it is clear that some do use it in what is called cybervetting, i.e. to rule out applicants who they feel don't meet the organisation's culture and values on the basis of things that have been published online.

Another key issue in the sector is the extent to which organisations need to look beyond their immediate requirements in recruitment. This issue can be separated into two parts. The first part has been of concern for decades and considers how organisations balance their assessment between looking at past behaviour and potential for future behaviour. This discussion centres on how much previous performance indicates future performance and whether it is preferable to assess what a candidate could potentially do in the future. For example, if someone has driven for years then immediately they may be a better driver. However, a personality selection test may show that a current non-driver would be better in the long run. The other aspect of this issue concerns to what extent the organisation should focus on their immediate operation and to what extent on their longer-term needs. In practical terms they need to decide whether to focus on the KSAs established for this specific role, with what it involves at this point in time or to be more future focused about what long-term they may desire from this employee. In some respects strengths-based interviewing is a means for being more future focused. Ryan and Ployhart (2014) argue future focus requires more than looking at the applicants' KSAs differently, though; it requires considering organisational performance at different levels, not just at the individual's level.

The final issues considered in this section are both current and perennial. That no satisfactory solution has so far been found indicates the complexity involved in both. The first concerns the problems in assessing on-the-job performance by applicants because this average performance can differ significantly from the maximal performance that most selection tools tap into. There are many variables influencing average performance. The one most researched is motivation. Attempts to tap this have, to a great extent, driven the increase in personality measurement as part of the selection process. Other strands of research have considered whether additional KSAs need to be considered beyond direct job performance. For example, team focus, the willingness to engage in organisational citizenship behaviours or competitiveness. Ultimately, maximal performance in high stakes assessment situations doesn't fully correlate with everyday performance though. The second current yet perennial problem concerns the measurement of traits, skills or abilities which are hard to quantify. Innovation and creativity are good examples of these more abstract KSAs. Assessments currently used tap either personality characteristics known to correlate, e.g. openness to experience and extraversion, or they measure creativity in dealing with a specific problem in a specific situation. Neither method is sufficiently valid to accurately predict these traits on the job, when required. Therefore this remains a significant area for research, investigation and – ironically – creativity and innovation.

SUMMARY

In this chapter we have explored the criteria involved in creating a selection process; the stages of the selection process; and mechanisms for evaluating the process used as well as consideration of the specific assessment tools used. We have also considered some of the issues currently of interest to those working in this field. Throughout the chapter, assessment and selection have been explored in the context of ideal scenarios. Psychologists will aim to operate according to the six criteria described when designing selection processes and aspire to engage with all stages of the recruitment cycle. However, real-world practices can be messy and complex, and individual psychologists may not control each stage of the process and frequently have to build on practices which already exist or miss a stage out. Most often the elements which are skimped are evaluation and job design. Unfortunately this can mean a psychologist designing assessment methods on faulty job analysis or never establishing whether a particular process works. In these ways the work can be frustrating. However, this frustration is mitigated by knowing that the system developed is the most fair it can be. Who is employed, and who is promoted has major impact on society culturally, politically, economically and socially, and so psychologists working in this field can rightfully feel that their work makes a difference in the world. However, one must not conflate an optimal process with a perfect one, and everyone working in this field should be mindful that no process is perfect.

As selection processes increasingly become automated, using quantitative measures and objective assessments, they can be mistaken for perfect assessment tools. It must always be remembered that there is no perfect measure. Noon is critical about selection methods, arguing that they don't deal with long-standing oppression, and asserts:

> A pseudo-scientific rationalism permeates selection processes, so where candidates are assessed through 'objective' means, such as aptitude tests or work samples, there is likely to be more trust in the measures produced by the assessment method – although the tests themselves may be flawed or lack high predictive validity for the particular job in question.
>
> (Noon, 2010, p. 732)

This is an important point for, as there is no one perfect measure, there is no one ideal candidate. Whoever fits the role best depends on your positioning. Noon is not advocating a less rational selection process but rather a move to view selection as part of a larger issue in employment. A specific conundrum can illustrate this point. Would it be better for an organisation to hire an employee who fits well within the current team or one who is substantially different in approach, beliefs and personality to 'shake the team up'? Diversity in organisation concerns gender, race, age, ethnicity, sexual orientation but also many more personal variables than those enshrined in legislation.

RECOMMENDATIONS FOR FURTHER READING

Highhouse, S., Doverspike, D., and Guion, R. (2016). *Essentials of Personnel Assessment and Selection*. London: Routledge.

Nikolaou, I., and Oostrom, J. (2015). *Employee Recruitment, Selection and Assessment*. London: Psychology Press.

Wigdor, A., and Sackett, P. (2016). Employment testing and public policy: The case of the General Aptitude Test Battery. In H. Schuler, J. Farr and M. Smith (eds), *Personnel Selection and Assessment: Individual and Organizational Perspectives*. London: Routledge, pp. 183–204.

LEARNING, TRAINING AND DEVELOPMENT

INTRODUCTION

Most organisations have structured training and development plans for their employees, even if these only reflect the need to induct and get new employees up to speed. Often these focus on training as if this were the outcome of the process. Organisational psychologists focus instead on the learning: i.e., the behavioural change in the employee rather than the act of training. The changed emphasis is significant as it means that learning can be considered in its broadest sense. Organisational psychologists, as a result look at conscious and unconscious learning, classroom-based as well as on-the-job learning, and learning which goes against the organisation's interests or stated plans as well as that which is actively facilitated.

Psychologists are not the only professionals working in this field. There are many other roles which overlap and complement. For example, human resource professionals may specialise as a training and development officer, and management consultants often focus on this area. It is also important to note that this aspect of the occupational psychology role is different from teaching. In teaching, a general change is sought in the learner: to become a better citizen, a more critical thinker or to understand the world differently, for example. The aim in teaching is usually to generate changes in ways of thinking.

DOI: 10.4324/9781315169880-3

In training the focus is on immediate or short-term behaviour change. Belief changes may occur alongside, for example in leadership development programmes, but it is the changed behaviour which is critical, and this is how the success of training and development interventions is judged. In this chapter we look at organisational training and development as if they were being used transparently. However, it should be noted that training can also be employed as a mechanism for rewarding staff or in an attempt to solve wider organisational issues. These aims are outside the scope of this chapter.

TRAINING AND DEVELOPMENT CYCLE

The training and development cycle should be a continual loop in which training needs are identified, the most effective systems are designed to meet those needs, training is delivered and then evaluation occurs feeding back into a new analysis of need. However, Salas et al. (2012) show that organisations often skip training needs analysis (TNA) and attempt to design or deliver interventions with no baseline from which to measure, or understanding of the needs of the organisation. In this way evaluation is near impossible, and critical needs can be left unmet. In addition, failure to move systematically through the stages of the cycle mean that active harm can be done too (Davies, 1972) as inappropriate training can be worse than no training.

Training needs analysis is the process of assessing what training needs to focus on, as well as what parameters or limitations could hinder learning. There are three key foci organisational psychologists have in TNA: organisational analysis, task analysis and person analysis. Organisational analysis involves looking at the organisation at a macro level and what it hopes to achieve. Typical starting points would be mission and vision statements and consideration of any weaknesses apparent. It is important that such weaknesses are contextualised by looking at the mission, vision and values of the organisation though: they may not be something which they feel need to be addressed. For example, Ryanair's CEO contextualised reports of poor customer service by the organisation as something that customers should endure because they offer low prices. In contrast an organisation which is already reported to have good customer service, such as Lush, may want to maximise this reputation and focus on this as part of their training strategy. So it is not always the case that training is to target weaknesses at the organisational level. When conducting organisational analysis it is also important to consider legal requirements for training (for example in relation to terrorism prevention, data protection or health and safety) as well as the resources available for implementing training and which employees should be the focus of development.

TNA is also conducted in a more focused way as job analysis (also referred to as task analysis) and person analysis. Job analysis should only be undertaken once organisational analysis has been completed. It involves looking at the specific activities which are required in different roles within an organisation. This is also something completed during recruitment and selection so it may be there is learning that can be transferred across. Please see Chapter 2 for more details on this process. Finally person analysis should be undertaken. This process establishes where the learning gaps are for an individual. Person analysis should focus on the knowledge, skills and experiences the individual needs to perform their current role effectively. A range of existing data sets can feed into this such as appraisal records, customer feedback and sales data. It may be that individuals are also asked to undertake testing as well, for example a sales associate may be given a test about the key products they are selling to establish if they have a knowledge gap.

When conducing TNA the focus is often on what employees need to learn to be successful in their current roles. Most organisation also recognise the importance of future focus as well. This should be considered at each point of TNA. It should include: longer-term strategies of the organisation; potential changes to individual roles and new roles; and personal interests of the individual. It is important the training plans consider where the organisation and individual want to be in the future, not just what they need to do to be successful where they are at this point in time. Finally, whilst gathering data on what is required in a development plan through TNA it is also helpful to gather demographic information about potential trainees. Goldstein and Ford (2001) argue this should include information on education level, technological skills, motivation level and personality traits such as conscientiousness. These factors then facilitate the next stage of the cycle, training design.

Training design should focus on how best to maximise learning transfer for the group of individuals identified. It is important to consider learners as individuals throughout the design process to ensure their individual differences are accommodated. It is also at this stage that critical decisions should be made about how learning and development are facilitated, critically whether this will be through formal or informal training, whether it will be face to face or online/virtual and whether it involves real scenarios or simulations. The designer also needs to consider whether certification or accreditation of learning is necessary. Whilst evaluation is considered as a specific discrete step later in this cycle the actual design of evaluation strategies should occur during training design to ensure appropriate data is gathered at each stage.

The first consideration in training design is whether it is necessary to have formal sessions. Sometimes this is a requirement for legally mandated training or to meet the requirements of accreditations. For example, catering staff are mandated to have completed food hygiene certificates, and higher education institutes in the UK are assessed on percentage of staff with teaching qualifications. However, informal development plans can be effective for learning transfer, for example a new office worker may learn to take service meetings and take minutes by shadowing existing staff. Design is still relevant as they need to be timetabled to be with appropriate staff; informed of the development plan so they are focused and motivated to learn; and paired with people who have the relevant knowledge and are prepared to facilitate that learning transfer. Where formal training is to be delivered, consideration needs to be made as to when and how this occurs. Online and virtual training environments have benefits for allowing participants to attend flexibly around other work commitments. They also mean that individuals can potentially access training most relevant to their personal circumstances, e.g. existing knowledge level or preferred pace of study. Computer-assisted instruction also allows for immediate specific feedback on performance, and systems can be built to force learners to cover material in a specific order. Other self-access learning such as workbooks should also be considered and can often be appropriate in environments where computers are not readily available. For example, a gas engineer could use a workbook between jobs to learn about new legislation. Workbooks are increasingly side-lined in favour of online materials, but the personal circumstances of the individual learner should be considered, including preferences and familiarity with technology use. A workbook can be studied on a bus ride to work. Not all employees will have the technology or skills to use this time to study online. This is not to say face-to-face learning no longer has a place. This type of training can increase motivation as learners work together. There can be economies of scale and practical benefits in running group training sessions as well, particularly when learning involves working cooperatively on projects. Face-to-face sessions are particularly beneficial for skills training as they allow immediate trialling or and feedback on skill use in action.

In designing skills development sessions, there is a further decision: whether to use real or simulated scenarios, resources and situations. Simulations allow low risk training to occur as the outcomes don't have real-world implications. It is fine to train in real scenarios when the potential dangers are low. For example, checkout operators can be trained on the job with the real resources. They are likely to be slower than trained staff but there is no real risk to this scenario. In contrast medical professionals need to start their training in simulated environments to minimise risk to real people. Cost may be a factor in whether real or simulated scenarios are used as well. Whilst new pilots usually start in simulations, when they are being trained for larger aircraft, they do so on real flights as the costs of running training flights are too prohibitive. If using simulations then they should be made with as high fidelity as possible, i.e. similarity to the real situation, as this impacts learning transfer.

Learning transfer is affected by a range of factors both in training design and in training delivery. Motivation, similarity of scenario to real situation and opportunity to use skills learnt are all key variables that impact learning transfer and so must be considered in training delivery. Motivation to learn is affected by a range of factors, only some of which are within the trainer's control. These include: degree of conscientiousness, level of self-efficacy felt in relation to the task and locus of control (Colquitt et al., 2000). The former is outside the trainer's control, but the latter two can be impacted by how training is approached, in particular the feedback which is given on performance (this should be supportive but honest) as well as how training is framed in relation to how it can be implemented in the workplace. Similarity of scenario to real situation is broader than whether a simulation has fidelity: if participants can't see how the training links to what has to be learned then learning transfer is affected. A simple solution is to ensure that learning outcomes are shown to participants and there is constructive alignment between what is to be learned, how it is being learned and how it is to be tested. Where simulations are used it is the trainer's responsibility to ensure high fidelity is achieved. For example, in training battlefield medics it is important not just to simulate the physical actions the medic will have to undertake with realistic dummies but also to mimic the noise and smells of such a scenario. If these are absent from the learning situation, then it impacts the ability of the trainee to recall during the real situation. Generating similar scenarios can require quite ingenious and creative solutions from trainers. These range from the high-tech, for example anatomically accurate models for midwives to practise on made of materials which simulate human skin and tissue, to the very low-tech, for example ensuring music is playing and a conversation is ongoing nearby a trainee retail operative, as happens in their real sales environment.

The next element of this cycle is evaluation. Note this is a point in the cycle rather than an endpoint. This is because the evaluation should feed directly back into the next round of TNA and not be a fixed end point. Evaluation will be considered in the later section. Suffice it to say here that good evaluation at this point depends on having taken baseline measures earlier in the cycle to provide comparison.

EXAMPLE: PROBLEMS WITH COPYING TRAINING INTERVENTIONS

ABC company run a chain of call centres as well as retail stores. They notice that their senior staff are not very diverse in either of the organisations and that they often have to hire people from outside the organisation for senior roles which impacts morale. So, they do a careful needs analysis to establish what the problem might be in the retail chain. They establish that when their employees apply for promotion, they often don't have the required skills. As it is specific groups who are underrepresented, they design and run one leadership training programme specifically for women and another for black people and people from either Indian or Pakistani ethnic groups. The choices of participants for the programmes reflected careful needs analysis of the staff working at all levels in the retail organisation as well as consideration of the local population makeup. After the programme has been running for two years, they see an upturn in selection of managers from within the organisation and more diversity in their senior team. The success of this intervention gives them confidence to extend the programmes to the call centre side of the business.

Because the intervention was already shown to work, they fail to undertake a training needs analysis or consider the context of the call centre and simply begin to run the same training programmes in the new organisation. After running the programmes for two years they find that the diversity in the senior staff hasn't change and that staff who have undertaken the training programme are more likely to leave the organisation than other staff. They interview staff who have taken the programme and find out that they are demoralised and likely to be looking for work elsewhere. The reasons are that the call centre environment is much flatter than the retail chain. Essentially there are only three levels of staff: call handler, supervisor and senior manager with the ratio of 240:40:1. This contrasts with the retail organisation which had checkout operators, supervisors, store managers, regional managers and senior managers in a ratio of 240:36:12:4:1. In the call centre people completing the training had no opportunity to practise their skills afterwards, and the jump between levels was too great without having had experience in other roles, and so even when one of the very few senior positions became vacant current staff were still not able to successfully apply.

LEARNING TRANSFER

Learning transfer refers to both knowledge transfer and resulting behavioural change which occurs as a result of that knowledge transfer. It is quite possible that learning can occur with no changed behaviour. This is not regarded as learning transfer in an organisational context. Several terms have specific meaning in this context, so definitions are important. Learning refers to the process of acquiring knowledge or skills. Training is one of the processes of facilitating that learning. Training implies there is a conscious effort both on the part of the learner and another person who acts as trainer. Development, in this context, refers to the process of learning without a specific trainer. It implies growth on a personal level and changes in thinking: more than knowledge acquisition. Development can occur simply from being in a facilitative environment with no conscious effort expended to make it occur. For example, an employee may develop diplomacy skills by being collocated with someone who uses those skills daily. This is not to imply that no design is involved. The learning and development adviser may have consciously paired those staff together. It is not necessary that either staff is aware of this though. Placements such as this for development purposes are sometimes large scale, for example, in job rotation programmes. In this technique staff are moved between different roles or departments to learn from being in that environment, either with or without supplemental training. This is a feature of many graduate training programmes. One of the benefits of such programmes is that active practice is built in: this is known to aid learning transfer.

Active practice refers to the process of using the skills and knowledge which have been given during training to embed that learning. It is easy to see that learning to swim, drive or ride a bike requires such practice, but transfer of more abstract learning also depends on opportunities to practise. In a classroom scenario this can be achieved by building in tests; encouraging the generation of notes; or asking participants to cascade their learning to others in their team. All of these behaviours force the active engagement with the material and so embed learning. Active practice can be problematic when developing future-focused training programmes though, for example, leadership training. An organisation may recognise the need to develop future leaders to meet projected needs. They then build specific training programmes to facilitate this skill development. The training can allow immediate transfer of knowledge such as negotiation skills, tactics for listening or problem solving. Unfortunately, many trainees then revert to their usual jobs with no opportunity to use the skills, and so they eventually become extinct. Trainers need to consider how initial practice is best organised and how it can be used to ensure learning is retained over time, until required. To do so, it is important that training and development functions are integrated into other organisational activities to allow space, time and opportunity to practise learned skills by, for example, taking leadership of a small project or acting up for someone on leave from work. Practice should be spaced differently depending on task type. For simple tasks practice is most effective when it is done in larger blocks with shorter rest periods. Tasks of this type include operating simple machinery and serving customers. Optimal learning transfer will occur if employees learn these tasks just before they are required to use them. Where a task is more complex, such as counselling an individual, or using a complex computer program, then practice is most effective in shorter bursts with longer spacing in between. An alternative method is to break more complex tasks into much smaller sub-units. Participants who are less intelligent or less educated may particularly benefit from this approach. However, it is important to establish that there are no qualitative differences between the task in units and the task as a whole. For example, counsellors need to learn a range of techniques: active listening; paraphrasing; summarising; directing and action planning. Some can be learnt as sub-units. Action planning is performed at a specific point in the counselling cycle and can be independently learned. It is not, in contrast, helpful for a trainee counsellor to learn to summarise independently of active listening as the skills need to be used in conjunction when working, and the scenario has lower fidelity if they are allowed to practise by focusing only on one aspect. Such focus means other aspects of the real situation are not represented, for example the cognitive load involved, or that the situation is continuously changing.

It is not just task differences which impact learning transfer. Individual differences also affect whether development opportunities are successful. Personality traits such as openness to experience and extraversion are linked to learning particularly through informal routes. Individual differences impact many facets of learning transfer in all learning situations though. Colquitt et al.'s (2000) meta-analysis identified age, anxiety and conscientiousness as key factors impacting learning transfer, whilst Sitzman and Ely's (2011) meta-analysis found that the personal characteristics having the greatest effect were feelings of self-efficacy, persistence and effort expended. These factors have been explored extensively in the field of goal-setting research which indicates the importance of setting targets for learning which have meaning for the individual, and which the individual believes is within their capacity to achieve to maximise learning. These factors then predict motivation and persistence. This can be difficult for the trainer who may have to provide differentiated learning outcomes for different participants or otherwise differentiate the learner experience.

This can be done by providing extension material to some participant or different roles in activities such as role play, such that different skills are developed. Differentiation needs to be carefully managed though so that participants don't see it as patronising, unfair or otherwise inappropriate. Wherever possible, learners should be grouped to have common characteristics to limit these effects.

Learners are sometimes grouped according to what is termed different learning styles. The concept of learning styles is very popular amongst non-psychologist trainers. The most famous example of learning styles is Honey and Mumford's model which states that individuals learn best when using their preferred learning style. The styles were built on Kolb's model of the reflective learner, and this theoretical underpinning is used by proponents to give credibility to the idea. The four styles are: activist, theorist, relector and pragmatist. Proponents suggest that different learning activities should be offered for the different styles, for example activitists may prefer problem solving, role play and discussion whereas reflectors like self-analysis questionnaires, observing and receiving feedback. There is little support for the notion of learning styles: learning in preferred style has not been shown to increase learning transfer (e.g. Willingham et al., 2015). One reason for its popularity in training situations, in particular in public sector organisations, is perhaps because it seems intuitive that enjoyment of learning would lead to greater learning, even if this is not the case. In addition, it may be easier to persuade people to participate in non-compulsory training if it matches their preferences, hence it remains popular.

Feedback to learners can be critical to success, with Hattie's (1987) synthesis of meta-analyses of student learning concluding that it was the most important single effect on learner achievement. Despite this it is not always available to learners, particularly if they are simply shadowing another member of staff or doing less formal training. When engaging in a formal training programme, learners will receive feedback as a form of extrinsic information. This allows them to modify their behaviours to achieve the desired outcome. However, for the workplace, learners need to go beyond displaying the required behaviour during assessment. They need to be able to use intrinsic information, that is, data which means they can self-correct behaviour every day during their work. For example, a machine operator might need to be able to hear and recognise cue noises from their machine. A customer service operative might need to recognise signs a customer is becoming anxious or aggressive. When starting to learn, students may need feedback from a trainer or supervisor to help them recognise these cues. As they improve, they will be able to work unaided. Feedback can come from other sources than a trainer though: from the outputs of a learner's efforts (trial and error) or from supervisors. Supervisors can be helpful both in providing feedback and role modelling desired behaviours (Blume et al., 2010). It is worth noting that learners may also receive feedback which harms their learning. This is particularly problematic when a taught behaviour does not fit with an organisational or team culture. For example, a learner may receive safety training and return to the workplace correctly wearing their protective equipment and ensuring guards are in place. They may then receive feedback from peers that their taught processes are inappropriate or undesired because they are uncool, time-consuming or such like and revert to unsafe practices. However, peer feedback can also be supportive and help learners to use their new skills and knowledge (Pidd, 2004). This is an example of how different areas of work psychology operate together so that, when designing training activities, the psychologist should also consider wider organisational issues, rather than the problem in isolation. The organisation may regard poor safety practices as a result of lack of training or understanding of good practices. The initial TNA by the psychologist may uncover that it is in fact a culture issue which will not be resolved by training though.

For psychologists assessing training need and designing interventions there are a range of additional issues to consider in a diverse and globalised workforce. It is probable that not all potential trainees are starting from the same base point. This may be in relation to their level of existing knowledge, skill or education. It might also be in relation to their experiences of different styles of learning. Employees from different countries or different professions may have experienced different educational techniques. For example, nurses traditionally have a lot of reflection in their training, whereas lawyers have more experience of drilling facts. This can influence how quickly each staff member can learn through what is potentially a new technique. This is particularly important to consider when mixed teams are to be trained as they may require different methods. Pre-training tasks can both help all learners with training transfer and ensure that trainees all start at the same knowledge level (Blume et al., 2010). They can also be effective in establishing if some potential trainees are not engaged. Learning transfer is unlikely to happen in unengaged learners.

EXAMPLE: DEVELOPMENT FOR SUCCESSION PLANNING

ABC recognise the problems with their previous approach and have now looked more fully at the call centre environment and how they might approach training there. They have decided to move away from the previous leadership training programme which included many staff and work in a more focused way with fewer staff members who have the potential to make the move from call handler to supervisor to senior manager. In so doing they are able to offer development opportunities which would not be available to lots of staff members.

Succession planning is an approach in which the organisation recognises where they may have vacancies in the coming 1–3 years and works directly with some staff members to prepare them for those roles. It is important when succession planning that there is no unfair discrimination, and that selection is done according to the law (see Chapter 2). So ABC look to see which senior staff are most likely to retire or otherwise leave the organisation and then assess existing staff to see who could be trained to fill those roles. Previously they had not considered the existing knowledge and skills of call handlers before allowing them to join the leadership programme. With the new route they work directly with staff who already have other specialist skills or knowledge, targeting in particular those who are not using their current skills fully. This means they are more likely to be able to make the large jump from supervisor to senior manager, without intermediary roles. This may be, for example, an accountancy graduate who is working in the non-graduate call handler role or someone who has already run their own business but is working as a call handler so they have steady hours whilst their children are dependent. The development programme ABC implement involves these staff members initially shadowing senior staff before gradually spending part of the week working on more senior projects to build skills and experience. This means that they are working towards a vacancy which is likely to exist when they are ready to take it up.

EVALUATION

An evaluation strategy should be planned in at the design phase of the intervention. It is vital that the relevant metrics of success are pre-decided, otherwise all interventions can be viewed as successful. The metric of success should be tied to the original issue that was identified when it was established that training was the right intervention. For example, staff are seen to be using unsafe techniques in a factory, so training is organised. The appropriate metric of success would then be whether safe techniques are being used post-training intervention. There will be existing metrics to use to assess this such as accident records or rates. However, for other forms of training there may be no existing metric. For example, it may be determined that all staff will benefit from training in use of a computer package and so there is no record of their existing ability. Therefore, a baseline check of ability should be conducted prior to training. This will also ensure that training design is based on learner need and that learners are not working on skills they already possess. In this way evaluation is some-thing that should be intrinsic to the entire intervention, though it is often regarded as a bolt-on for after training ends. For longer periods of training then multiple evaluation points should be used as there is no benefit in using staff time and resource in continuing a programme which is not effective. A good evaluation strategy will also build in checks on skill decay and consider when learning is actually needed. For some interventions, for example, leadership training, it may be some time before the learned skills are used, and Arthur et al.'s (1998) meta-analysis demonstrated that skill decay is correlated with lack of use of skill post-training. So, it is not appropriate to assess learning immediately post-training, but rather at the point at which the skill is required by the organisation. This meta-analysis also showed that there was faster decay for cognitive rather than physical tasks, some-thing to be considered in evaluation design.

The most popular model of evaluation is that of Kirkpatrick (1994) which will be the only theoretical model considered here due to space. This model lays out four potential levels of evaluation. Table 3.1 explains these and the associated issues with each level. The first two levels reflect benefit to the individual learner whilst the latter two levels reflect benefit to the organisation.

TABLE 3.1 Kirkpatrick's levels of evaluation

Level	What is being measured	Possible strategy	Challenges
1	Reaction to learning: Did participants enjoy the activity and/or feel it was helpful?	Participants complete 'happy sheets' (short questionnaire asking about experience)	Low validity of data
2	Extent of learning	Assessments of knowledge or skills before and after intervention	Difficult for complex learning or if attempting to change attitudes
3	Behaviour in the workplace	Observation of workers in the workplace	Can be expensive and time-consuming to undertake
4	Results or outputs of learning	Likely to use pre-existing metrics such as accident logs, efficiency rates, number of complaints, etc.	Can be difficult to make clear links between the intervention and the metric – they are not always closely tied and there may be other factors which impact

Sugrue and Rivera (2005) found that the usage of the different levels of evaluation decreased dramatically from levels one to four with 91%, 54%, 23%, and 8% using each level respectively. Given the particular issues with validity with level one evaluation it is problematic that evaluation is given such little emphasis in the process. A more recent Chartered Institute of Personnel and Development report (CIPD, 2021) found that 24% of organisations conducted no systematic evaluation at all of their interventions though the figure is impacted by lower evaluation by smaller and medium-sized enterprises of which 35% conducted no evaluation. This may reflect the fact that work psychologists account for only a small number of the designers of such interventions with many other professionals also working in this area. The model has been criticised for focusing only on the benefits within the organisation without considering wider benefits. Models such as Birdi's TOTADO model and Warr et al.'s (1970) CIRO model address this, yet Kirkpatrick's remains the one used 77% of the time in academic evaluations (Hilbert et al., 1997). Various additions have been proposed to Kirkpatrick's approach, with Kaufman and Keller (1994) suggesting societal impact should be a fifth level and various authors suggesting return on investment be included.

Return on investment (ROI) is a concept used for a range of psychological and business interventions. It is essentially a process by which the expense incurred in conducting an intervention is calculated relative to the financial benefits of the intervention. In the case of training, it would be worked out as:

$$ROI = \frac{TRAINING\ BENEFITS - TRAINING\ COSTS}{TRAINING\ COSTS} \times 100$$

However, working out the benefits gained from training can be difficult. They might come from improvements in productivity, but they may also result from fewer accidents, fewer legal or disciplinary cases or fewer machine stoppages or periods of downtime. Establishing the training costs can be easier, but it is important to think beyond the immediate costs of hiring trainer, producing materials and booking venues. There are additional costs in preparing the programme as well as in the staff time for attending the course and the knock-on effects of these staff not being in role. For less formal interventions such as work shadowing the costs of both the staff member undertaking the shadowing should be counted as well as the reduced efficiency of the staff member who is facilitating their learning who will be operating at reduced capacity as they explain the different tasks being undertaken.

EXAMPLE: EVALUATING ABC'S DIFFERENT INTERVENTIONS USING KIRKPATRICK'S MODEL

	Leadership programme in call centre	Leadership programme in retail company	Development programme in call centre
Level 1: Did participants like the programme/ believe it to be beneficial?	Yes, programme was enjoyable Result of evaluation: *keep running intervention*		

(Continued)

(*Continued*)

Level 2: Participants' skill level is tested in simulations at the end of the course	Participants can demonstrate the required skills Result of evaluation: *keep running intervention*	
Level 3: Is the required behaviour observed in the workplace?	No, there is no opportunity for participants to lead or demonstrate skills which were taught Result of evaluation: *cannot judge effectiveness of intervention*	Yes, participants can lead on different projects and demonstrate skills which were taught Result of evaluation: *keep running intervention*
Level 4: Desired output of learning – are participants sufficiently skilled to progress to senior positions?	No, participants are unable to take up new positions due to skill decay and inappropriate participant selection Result of evaluation: *stop intervention*	Yes, increase in participants taking up senior positions Result of evaluation: *keep running intervention*
Level 5: Return on investment – did the intervention save or earn the company extra revenue?	Company lost money as there was increased staff turnover Result of evaluation: *stop intervention*	Company saved money as the cost of the intervention was less than the cost of externally recruiting staff Result of evaluation: *keep running intervention*

It is worth noting that all of this evaluation focuses only on the impact of the intervention on the desired outcomes. There are likely to be a range of other outcomes from training or development interventions. Examples are increased morale as staff feel that the organisation cares about their long-term interests or decreased productivity, temporarily, as new skills are practised in the workplace and people become proficient in different ways of working.

CURRENT ISSUES IN THE SECTOR

Work psychology is a continuously evolving sector because the world of work is continuously evolving. In a VUCA world (volatile, uncertain, complex and ambiguous) it is hard to predict what the next big issues might be in a sector. With regard to learning, training and development there are a few key issues which are impacting already, however. These concern how technology is used in this sector, the role of massive open online courses (MOOCs) and who is ultimately responsible for being work ready: the individual employee, the state or employers. We will consider these issues in turn here.

Technology can facilitate training. It has the potential to allow mentoring at a distance, to use realistic simulations for learning and to give economies of scale in producing materials, for example with web access rather than print copies of learning resources. However, there are risks in using increasingly sophisticated pieces of soft- and hardware that some employees are left behind or that training becomes less effective because of technical problems, trainer capability or trainee competency or willingness to engage with new methods. Most people can remember a situation where a teacher or trainer struggled to connect to an online video, present the correct slides, etc., and Covid lockdowns have shown that even after years of online meetings people still forget basics about switching microphones on and off. Increasingly sophisticated pieces of hardware can allow trainees to use virtual reality to tour their new workplace and use paddles to interact with items in there. Realistic physical models can allow trainee pilots to fly simulated journeys, trainee midwives to deliver simulated babies and trainee firearms officers to respond to perceived threats. However, much of the technological development relies on keen changemakers – individuals who pioneer the use of a new system. When evaluations are done it is typically with such forerunners and their pilot projects. In the new phases of a project, it is the most enthusiastic trainers and trainees who are used with the newly purchased technologies which have not yet developed faults and with high levels of technical support. Later users of the systems may have other problems with confidence, self-efficacy in their use, breakdowns in the technology and less support. It is sometimes assumed that participants want high levels of technology, and the metaphor of digital native has been used to describe people, born after about 1980, who have grown up with technology and so are assumed to be able to use it effectively and intuitively. Such individuals have now been in the workplace for nearly a quarter of a century, and so we are not far from the position where the majority of employees are so-called digital natives. However, the concept has been somewhat misunderstood with the assumption that digital natives magically understand all technologies and do not need to learn how to use them. In fact, the concept is more that digital natives have a level of confidence in beginning to interact and to try to problem solve when issues arise. So work psychologists and other designers of learning should, when developing systems, ensure that both learners and those facilitating that learning have the skills and knowledge to use a system, as well as a feeling of self-efficacy to attempt to problem solve and not assume familiarity with systems which are new. Whilst it is helpful to consider the cohort effect of digital natives when designing for different age groups, it is important to acknowledge this is not a fixed category and that most digital 'immigrants' in the workplace will have, by now, had most of their working life using such technologies. For all staff it is the degree of confidence and self-efficacy which impacts, rather than their year of birth.

The rise of MOOCs over the last twenty years has led to some grand predictions regarding the role they might play in the future. MOOCs are short courses, accessed online, with little or no learner feedback involved. They are designed so that they can run with minimal trainer intervention. Sometimes this means learners provide feedback to each other, or there are reflective activities or automated or self-marking. They are open in the sense that they are free to access to learners and so might initially seem like a beneficial resource to individual learners and organisations. Many are developed in higher education institutions by leading academics, and some have quite sophisticated platforms. For example, in the UK, the Open University developed the Open Learn platform which hosts nearly a thousand MOOCs available to learners from around the world. Because they are free to access and break learning into short chunks, it has been suggested they might disrupt the whole higher education system as well as the way in which vocational training is delivered. Using them for staff development can be problematic though. MOOC design can serve a range of functions such as to encourage enrolment onto other, paid-for courses, as such they are unlikely to be well tailored to the needs of workplace learners. There is a particular danger in their takeup by organisations in the absence of full training needs analyses and mapping of how these may fit organisational needs. They are particularly attractive post-pandemic lockdown as employees are more used to online work and training budgets have been significantly reduced (CIPD, 2021). They are also likely to be attractive to individual employees who are focusing on their own learning and development needs either within or outside their organisation.

The CIPD (2021) urge organisations to invest in training and development which is evidence based and specific to their organisation's current and future predicted needs. However, cuts in such budgets reflect a potential shift back to individuals being more responsible for their development than organisations. This is something which shifts over time, with organisations taking primary responsibility in the early and mid-20th century until by the 1980s and 1990s individuals were regarded as being responsible. The start of the 21st century saw a swing back to organisations recognising the value of highly trained staff and so taking greater responsibility for this. The last five years have shown decreased funding and greater focus on individuals taking responsibility for their own continuous professional development. In part, this reflects wider moves in career management and organisation structure. Individuals are increasingly likely to be working across multiple organisations, changing jobs more frequently in order to progress as organisation structures are flattened making promotions within more difficult. Organisations might ask 'what if we train such employees and they leave?' To which, a counter-question should be asked 'what if you don't train them and they stay?' There has also been a rise in the so-called protean or boundaryless careers where individuals are less loyal to individual organisations and pursue their intrinsic values in work. Ultimately this means that their professional development will be in line with their own interests, rather than an organisation's future needs. Whilst the idea of such non-traditional careers has been widely described in the academic literature, most workers are still in traditional models, and so whilst work psychologists need to consider the needs of boundaryless workers in training design, their needs shouldn't overwhelm those of the majority of staff on more traditional paths.

SUMMARY

This chapter considered the need to use the whole training and development cycle in order to plan and deliver effective training. It summarised the steps of this process firstly looking at training needs analysis and its component parts of organisational, task and person analysis. It then considered the main points in designing good training, exploring issues such as how to choose the right type of training or development opportunity, whether accreditation is desirable, how the intervention will fit with other work the employee needs to do, and whether development can involve real work or simulations.

Factors impacting learning transfer were then considered with exploration of what it means to have learnt something and a look at how long-term learning or behaviour change needs to be planned. The importance of practice was discussed, with the need for training designers to build in longer-term opportunities, particularly if the skills being developed are not in immediate demand in the organisation, or if the individual won't be using them, for example on a leadership development programme where the participant might not be in a leadership role for some time.

The effects of individual differences in learning transfer were then explored. This included a critique of the concept of learning styles and a consideration of the benefits of certain personality traits for learning, e.g., that openness to experience and extraversion were both correlated with effective learning. The difficulties of accommodating such differences in training design were then considered alongside a discussion of the benefits and importance of feedback to effective learning. The need for an evaluation strategy was then explored in some depth, with a more in-depth look at Kirkpatrick's evaluation model and its strengths and limitations. The final section explored what current issues were impacting work in this area. There was an exploration of how technology changes allowed new ways of working and delivering training and what risks this involved in terms of potentially disenfranchising some groups of staff. Finally, the impact of MOOCs was considered, and there was some discussion about who is responsible for ensuring staff are work ready: the staff themselves or organisations.

RECOMMENDATIONS FOR FURTHER READING

Johnson, A., and Proctor, R. (2016). *Skill Acquisition and Training*. London: Routledge.

Thornton, G., Mueller-Hanson, R., and Rupp, D. (2017). *Developing Organizational Simulations*. London: Routledge.

The *Journal of Vocational Education and Training* is an open-source resource which will allow you to see the current discussions in this field.

WELLBEING AT WORK

In this chapter we introduce the broad topic of wellbeing at work. The challenges of defining and measuring workplace wellbeing will be discussed, as well as why wellbeing is important and what some of its predictors can be. We then consider the opposite end of the wellbeing spectrum: work-related stress. Again, we discuss the different approaches to conceptualising and measuring this, as well as the outcomes associated with work-related stress at the individual and organisational level. The concept of work–life balance will be introduced followed by a discussion of the impact of technology on wellbeing at work. Finally, we explore the discipline of positive psychology and its relevance to wellbeing at work

WHAT IS WELLBEING?

It is likely that every person reading this will have a different answer to the question of what wellbeing is, as wellbeing is a highly subjective and personal experience. Perhaps because of this, conceptualisations and definitions of wellbeing can be unclear or 'conceptually muddy', and definitions of wellbeing that are driven by theory (rather than common sense definitions) are distinctly lacking.

Linked to this problem is that a lot of researchers have described what wellbeing *looks like*, rather than *defining it* (i.e. providing a

DOI: 10.4324/9781315169880-4

Table 4.1 Examples of the range of definitions of wellbeing

Definitions of wellbeing
Three interrelated components: life satisfaction, pleasant affect, and unpleasant affect. Affect refers to pleasant and unpleasant moods and emotions, whereas life satisfaction refers to a cognitive sense of satisfaction with life' (Diener and Suh, 1997, p. 200)
'A global assessment of a person's quality of life according to his own chosen criteria' (Shin and Johnson (1978, p. 478)
'Well-being is more than just happiness. As well as feeling satisfied and happy, well-being means developing as a person, being fulfilled, and making a contribution to the community' (Marks and Shah, 2004, p. 2)

definite statement of the exact meaning of the term). For example, look at some of the proposed definitions of wellbeing below. Do these allow us to be really clear about what wellbeing is, and what it means for people?

So, clearly there are a range of ways in which wellbeing can be conceptualised. As regards what this means practically in the workplace, a key challenge for work psychologists is that, if we do not know what wellbeing is and there is no common understanding of its meaning, then trying to measure, monitor and improve it can be difficult.

The Chartered Institute of Personnel and Development suggest the following definition of wellbeing at work:

> Creating an environment to promote a state of contentment which allows an employee to flourish and achieve their full potential for the benefit of themselves and their organisation.
>
> *(CIPD, 2007, p. 21)*

This is in line with the positive psychology movement, which characterises psychology as being about trying not only to avoid illness, but to help people to grow and be the best, most content version of themselves possible. We will revisit this concept later on in this chapter, but for now we will focus on wellbeing in the workplace as about more than simply avoiding feeling 'bad'. We will conceptualise wellbeing at work instead as being about feeling energised, happy and fulfilled in one's job.

As a note on how conceptualisations of wellbeing differ from work health, the latter is a discipline of medicine which aims to prevent accidents and care for employees who are already unwell. This typically includes rehabilitation for musculoskeletal disorders or psychological ill health, health surveillance (e.g. vision or hearing testing), immunisations and so on. These areas are not typically the domain of work psychologists. In contrast, wellbeing is a concept that should be a consideration for all employees within a business (not just those who are already unwell or at risk of becoming so).

WHY IS WELLBEING AT WORK IMPORTANT?

Wellbeing is a hot topic, and countless books, blogs, social media posts and academic articles are published daily about the many facets of wellbeing. Unsurprisingly, wellbeing at work is no less in the spotlight, especially for younger generations (Generation Y/Millennials and Generation Z/Screenagers) who have higher expectations of benefits, promotions, work–life balance, purpose and intellectual challenges than the generations before them. The global pandemic of 2020 saw a shift in many people's attitude to work, as working from home became the norm across numerous sectors, and the term 'work–life balance' (discussed later in this chapter) took on a new meaning. Work psychologists therefore have a role to play in ensuring that organisations are providing the best environments to attract, retain and develop their staff in line with these new expectations, and also to help individuals understand the factors that impact on their own wellbeing at work to empower them to act upon them.

THE BUSINESS CASE FOR WELLBEING AT WORK

Put simply, employees who are happy, healthy and engaged at work are more productive, less likely to take sickness absence, and are less likely to leave their job. For these reasons, taking notice of, and aiming to improve, the wellbeing of employees can significantly impact a business' bottom line. Financially, the return on promoting employee wellbeing is likely to be well worth the investment, providing that the approach to doing so is evidence based and appropriate for the organisation's specific needs. This is because employees who have poor wellbeing are likely to cost the company a lot of money through being absent or less effective at work (we will cover this in more detail later in the chapter), whereas those who are well and happy can be productive and help the organisation be more efficient.

MEASURING WELLBEING AT WORK

One of the key roles of work psychologists is to define, measure and evaluate any interventions relating to the area that they have been brought in to support the organisation with. In the case of wellbeing, we have already discussed in this chapter how challenging it can be to define it – and this does not become any less complex when it comes to *measuring* wellbeing in the workplace. Table 4.2 outlines three of the most popular metrics used to identify areas of priority for wellbeing interventions in organisations, along with some of the strengths and weaknesses for each.

Although this table only covers some of the possible ways to collect data about employees' wellbeing, it is intended to demonstrate that no one method is perfect for gathering such information. Using a combination of methods to gain as much information from different sources

TABLE 4.2 Measures of wellbeing

Surveys		Absence Rates		Interviews	
Strengths	Weaknesses	Strengths	Weaknesses	Strengths	Weaknesses
Anonymous	Data usually quantitative (can lack detail)	Easy to obtain	Does not capture presenteeism	Provides rich data about individuals	Possible bias in who volunteers (only very dis/satisfied employees)
Cost-effective	Self-report, subject to bias	Easy to compare over time	Does not capture attitudes	Can help employees to feel more valued	Time-consuming/ requires expertise to analyse
Easy to compare over time	Respondents cannot clarify the meaning of questions, making answers less valid	Not self-report (more reliable)	Can be confounded with other reasons for absence	Respondents can clarify understanding and interpretation of questions	Less directly comparable over time

as possible is desirable, so that work psychologists can gain as full and accurate a picture about the state of wellbeing in the organisation as possible; however, doing so inevitably takes more time and therefore costs the organisation more money. Therefore, there is a 'trade-off' to be struck between cost efficiency and the richness and value of the data gathered (and in turn the likely suitability and effectiveness of any interventions put in place) – see Chapter 7 for more detail on this trade-off in practice.

We have discussed the breadth of the concept of wellbeing and how work psychologists might go about measuring it – along with the challenges associated with both of these things. Next, we will explore concepts that are associated with wellbeing at work.

RELATED CONSTRUCTS

Unsurprisingly, there are many factors that predict wellbeing at work to a greater or lesser extent, which will be discussed throughout this chapter. As wellbeing is such a broad area, the range of variables that can impact on it are enormous, and there are a number of associated, yet conceptually separate constructs that are often researched in conjunction with wellbeing, which are described in this section.

JOB SATISFACTION

The concept of job satisfaction has been addressed by many different researchers and is considered to be important in wellbeing research for two key reasons:

1. As a potential indicator of a person's psychological wellbeing or mental health.
2. Job satisfaction is often assumed to lead to motivation and good work performance.

One of the most widely used definitions in organisational research is Locke's (1976, p. 1300) who defined job satisfaction as a 'pleasurable or positive emotional state resulting from the appraisal of one's job or job experiences'. This definition clearly demonstrates how job dis/satisfaction can relate to an individual's subjective experience of wellbeing at work. But what impacts on whether people enjoy their job or not?

A PERSON'S GENERAL PERSONALITY OR DISPOSITION

There is strong evidence that some people are simply more satisfied with their jobs than others by their nature. In general, research suggests that high levels of the personality traits extraversion and conscientiousness tend to be associated with higher job satisfaction, whereas higher levels of neuroticism appear to be related to lower job satisfaction (Judge et al., 2002). Therefore, this dispositional approach to job satisfaction would suggest that individuals are predisposed to be satisfied or dissatisfied with their job, regardless of the characteristics of the job itself. Personality traits can be objectively measured by psychometric tests, as discussed in Chapter 2.

THE FEATURES OF A PERSON'S JOB

Another school of thought, however, suggests that it is not the individual so much as the intrinsic (fundamental) features of the job itself that drive people's satisfaction. Hackman and Oldham (1976) define these intrinsic features of work in five ways:

- Skill variety: the extent to which the tasks require different skills.
- Task identity: the extent to which an employee can complete a 'whole' piece of work.
- Task significance: the extent to which the work is perceived as influencing the lives of others.
- Autonomy: whether the worker has freedom within the job to decide how it should be done.
- Feedback: whether there is correct and precise information about how effectively the worker is performing.

As work psychologists, we cannot change employees' personality traits (as these are thought to be relatively stable over time) but it *is* possible to amend intrinsic aspects of the job to maximise wellbeing. Interventions attempting to improve wellbeing in workplaces very often focus on changing features of people's jobs for this reason.

ENGAGEMENT

Work engagement is generally defined in the literature as a positive, fulfilling work-related state of mind. It is a pleasurable experience for many workers that goes along with feelings of:

- Absorption: being so engrossed in one's work that it is difficult to 'let go' of tasks, and not noticing time passing.
- Vigour: high levels of energy and mental resilience while working.
- Dedication: feeling that one's work 'means something'; feeling inspired and welcoming challenges.

Research suggests that engaged employees put a lot of effort in their work because they identify with it. As a result, engagement is assumed to produce positive outcomes, both at the individual level (personal growth and development) as well as at the organisational level (performance quality).

WORK-RELATED STRESS

Arguably the opposite of wellbeing at work is work-related stress, which is another construct that has received much attention in the literature with numerous definitions and theories associated with it. This is a phenomenon that most people who have had a job can personally identify with. Unlike wellbeing more broadly, work-related stress has been defined, studied and measured using three distinct theory-driven approaches, which are outlined in brief below.

ENGINEERING APPROACH

Work-related stress is considered to be an aversive or noxious characteristic of the work environment. It is an independent variable (i.e. the environmental cause of ill health).

PHYSIOLOGICAL APPROACH

In the physiological approach, work-related stress is the physiological response to a threatening or damaging environment. It is a dependent variable (i.e. the outcome caused by a bad work environment).

PSYCHOLOGICAL APPROACH

Both the engineering and physiological approaches to studying work-related stress have been criticised for being overly simplistic and somewhat dated. For example, they are set within a relatively simple stimulus–response paradigm and so do not account for individual differences in the perceptual and cognitive processes that might underpin stress (i.e. what one person considers to be a noxious characteristic in a work environment may be perfectly pleasant for someone else). These models treat the person as somewhat passive, ignoring the important interactions between a person and their environment.

However, in the psychological approach work-related stress is considered to be a result of the *dynamic interaction* between the person and their work environment. This recognises that the interaction between a person and their work environment will mean that different people will respond to situations in different ways, and so what is stressful for one person will not necessarily cause stress for someone else. In addition, people will experience stress differently, due to the range of cognitive and emotional reactions it may cause.

CAUSES OF WORK-RELATED STRESS

Causes of stress are often conceptualised in the literature as *psychosocial risks*. A psychosocial risk is the risk of detriment to a worker's psychological or physical wellbeing arising from the interaction between the design and management of work. Examples may include:

- Level of pay
- High workload
- Insufficient workload
- Weak management
- Blame culture
- Lack of opportunity to progress
- Physical environment
- Poor workplace relationships
- Insufficient expertise.

Note of course that any of these causes of stress may be present at some times and not at others. Additionally, some of these causes or 'risks' may be unique to particular organisations, and risks might emerge or disappear as workplaces evolve and change over time. And, perhaps most importantly, risks may impact differently on different people at different times, and also interact with each other to generate higher levels of stress than the sum of each individual risk in isolation. Therefore, arguably the causes of work-related stress can be as individual and subjective as the experience of stress (or, on the other side, wellbeing) itself. Hence the challenges that work psychologists face trying to define and measure it in practice.

OUTCOMES OF WORK-RELATED STRESS

What does experiencing work-related stress actually mean in real terms for the wellbeing of individuals experiencing it, and the organisations they work within? The impact can reach many areas, so the below are some non-exhaustive examples.

INDIVIDUAL-LEVEL OUTCOMES OF WORK-RELATED STRESS

Psychological and Social Outcomes

Anxiety and depression are the two lead presenting complaints associated with stress. Similarly, burnout is a form of psychological distress which often results from experiencing work-related stress. Burnout is characterised as emotional exhaustion, depersonalisation or cynicism, and lack of personal accomplishment. There is evidence that work-related stress is also related to a decline in the quality of relationships with one's spouse, children and other family members.

Physiological and Physical Outcomes

There is a wealth of evidence that work-related stress can have serious and lasting impacts on employees' physical health, including cardiovascular disease. Other research portrays stress as causal to the onset of cancers and having an indirect role in worsening the disease and limiting recovery.

ORGANISATIONAL-LEVEL OUTCOMES OF WORK-RELATED STRESS

In 2013 the Health and Safety Executive estimated that in the United Kingdom, work-related stress caused workers to lose 10.4 million working days in 2011/12, with significant financial losses to employers. Any costs to employers will include expenses from all of the following.

Absenteeism

Given the evidence that work-related stress impacts negatively on both mental and physical health, it follows that at the organisational level this will translate to employees being absent from work due to ill health. Note that *not* taking time off when experiencing ill health due to work-related stress can lead to presenteeism, which is discussed below.

Turnover

There is a wealth of evidence spanning many years that documents the relationship between work-related stress and turnover (i.e. employees leaving the organisation) across numerous professions, although much of the literature has focused on nursing. This finding is perhaps unsurprising and provides support for the idea that characteristics of a job lead to work-related stress – or at least are perceived to – as individuals changing jobs do so in the hope that another role may be less stressful.

Presenteeism

Presenteeism can be defined as the reduction in an employee's performance as a result of health issues when they choose to attend work but are not able to perform at their normal capacity. Some researchers have argued that employees being present when unwell may be even costlier than absenteeism to employers.

EUSTRESS

From the evidence presented so far in this chapter, you may be concluding that work-related stress is always bad, with negative outcomes. But is this really the case? Perhaps you can think of times when you have been under some pressure and performed at your best, or felt a sense of achievement when you completed the task? Such experiences are in line with the theory of eustress (Selye, 1974). As shown in Figure 4.4, it is proposed that a certain amount of perceived stress

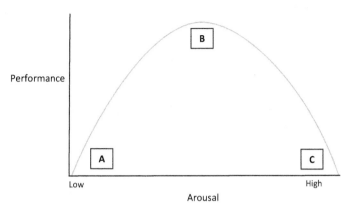

FIGURE 4.4 The Yerkes–Dodson curve

and physiological arousal is necessary to perform at the optimum level (B). However, if the level of arousal (stress) is too low (A), or alternatively, is perceived as exceeding one's capacity to cope (C), then distress results.

Further refinements of the definition of eustress have included using the term to mean the positive psychological response to a stressor, indicated by the presence of positive psychological states. Individuals experiencing eustress describe the experience in a variety of positive ways, including being totally focused, in a mindful state of challenge, a healthy state of aroused attention on the task, exhilaration, and being fully present.

In practice, however, this creates challenges for work psychologists and workplace managers. How can leaders draw upon the research on eustress to create 'eustressful' workplaces? Thinking back to the psychological definition of stress, we know that stress is the outcome of an individual's interaction with their environment; so what is 'eustressful' for one employee may be either under- or over-stressful for another.

WORK–LIFE BALANCE

Work–life balance is a term thrown around by many employees, managers and indeed work psychologists. It is often used colloquially to describe how much time employees spend at home versus at work – but as we will see in this section, theory and evidence show that there is much more to the concept than just hours at work.

DEFINITIONS OF WORK–LIFE BALANCE

As for many psychological phenomena, there is no single agreed-upon definition of work–life balance (WLB). However, common definitions include:

- Employees' satisfaction and good functioning of multiple roles among work and non-work (family or personal) domains.
- The extent to which an individual can function effectively and satisfactorily in both their work and family roles.
- WLB has also been divided into two separate constructs: work-to-family conflict (WFC) and family-to-work conflict (FWC). WFC occurs when work activities interfere with family responsibilities, and FWC occurs when family activities interfere with work responsibilities. Whichever direction the conflict is occurring in, the construct of WLB assumes an imbalance between *desired* and *actual* time, resources or effort spent on either work or family life.

THE SUBJECTIVITY OF WORK–LIFE BALANCE

Much of the literature on the topic of WLB has been concerned with the spillover of work into family life – however, family is only one aspect of life outside work, and for some individuals may not be a priority at all. Time for leisure, hobbies, exercise, socialising, and even 'mundane' things such as household chores and administrative tasks is also important. One criticism that can be levelled at the WLB research is that it has ignored several strata in society including those without families but with other significant responsibilities, such as caring for an elderly relative or pets.

A potentially more pressing issue is also apparent: is work distinguishable from 'life'? Is spending lots of time at work actually a 'problem'? The answer to these questions will differ from person to person. For some people, working long hours is in fact desirable and work–life imbalance can occur when people feel that they are working too little. These challenges of conceptualising and studying WLB were summarised by Eikhof et al. (2007), who claimed that the work–life balance debate is centred on questionable assumptions, mainly:

> that work is experienced as negative, with long working hours a particular problem; that 'life' can be equated with caring responsibilities, most particularly childcare, with the result that women are the primary target of work–life balance provisions; and that work and life are separable and in need of being separated.
>
> *(2007, p. 1)*

Take, for example, the question of gender relating to part-time work. Beham et al. (2018) found that in Europe, women in part-time work reported a much better WLB than men in similar working patterns, and the opposite to be true of those in full-time work (where men were more satisfied with their WLB). The researchers noted that the societal context plays an important role in this, with more gender-egalitarian countries showing higher WLB for men in part-time roles and females in full-time roles, compared to countries with low gender equality.

ORGANISATIONAL INTERVENTIONS FOR WORK–LIFE BALANCE

Organisational interventions for increasing WLB of employees relate to changes to the work environment, working practices and so on that are put in place for all employees, rather than being targeted specifically at individual employees. As outlined in the previous section, one of the potential pitfalls of this approach is that WLB will mean different things to different employees, so implementing a 'one size fits all' intervention which effectively improves all employees' WLB can be a significant challenge (if not nearly impossible) for work psychologists.

Research on organisational interventions around WLB typically falls into three main groups:

- Initiatives addressing working time and/or working hours
- Collaborative action research focused on improving workplace equity and performance levels (i.e. using the expertise of external consultants)
- Initiatives to embed WLB within organisational cultures.

A POSSIBLE INTERVENTION: COMPRESSED HOURS

Compressed hours is an example of an initiative addressing working time and/or working hours. This means that employees work the same number of hours per week as they originally did, but over fewer days.

In their review, Brough and O'Driscoll (2010) concluded that overall, compressed working weeks appear to be beneficial for enhancing WLB among workers, although more extended research timeframes are needed to determine whether initial benefits are maintained over time.

However, there are some key considerations that must take place before implementing compressed working hours as an approach to improve employees' WLB. A non-exhaustive list of these is provided below:

- May not be appropriate or even possible for all professions (e.g. an assembly line worker cannot continue to work after the assembly line has stopped for the night)
- Could be detrimental to the organisation's aims and mission statements
- Could be incompatible with employees' other responsibilities (e.g. collecting children from school)

May not be perceived as desirable by all employees.

OUTCOMES OF WORK–LIFE (IM)BALANCE

As discussed in the positive psychology section later in this chapter, much of the research has tended to focus on negative outcomes relating to work–life imbalance, rather than the positives associated with WLB being achieved. Nonetheless, where research does exist, work–family enrichment is conceptualised as a key positive outcome of WLB. Work–family enrichment focuses on the positive effects of work on family life (work-to-family enrichment) and family on the work life (family-to-work enrichment). Both work-to-family enrichment and family-to-work enrichment have been found to be positively related to:

- Physical health
- Mental health
- Family functioning
- Job satisfaction
- Organisational commitment.

There has been much research that shows the negative outcomes of a perceived work–life imbalance, including a range of physical ailments, mental health issues and increased burnout, stress and turnover intentions.

THE IMPACT OF TECHNOLOGY ON WORK–LIFE BALANCE

ALWAYS ON' CULTURE

It goes without saying that the ever-increasing sophistication, affordability and accessibility of technologies have the risk of further blurring the boundaries between work and non-work time. Access to work emails on their phone, for example, mean that many employees can complete their work or communicate with colleagues theoretically from anywhere, at any time.

One aspect of the workplace (and outside it) now is the 'always on' culture that exists in many organisations and roles. In today's society, many of us are working longer hours than ever before, and most of us spend as much, if not more, time at work as we do elsewhere. This is the case even though, by law in the UK, people cannot work more than 48 hours per week on average unless they voluntarily 'opt out' of this. Indeed, even before and after 'official' working hours, smartphones, laptops and tablets make checking work emails and contacting colleagues possible 24 hours a day, 7 days a week. If you're on a train before 9am, chances are that most people in your carriage are already checking and responding to emails and making work-related phone calls. As such, it can be argued that the boundaries between work and home life are blurred – perhaps to the extent of no longer existing. This leads to increased connectivity between employees and employers, which research has consistently shown makes the boundaries between work and home more permeable and suggests that technology is one of the major causes of work–home interference.

But blurring the boundaries between work and home lives is only problematic if the employer and/or employee perceive it to be, or it has associated negative outcomes. In this section we will briefly summarise the existing evidence in this area.

POSITIVE EFFECTS OF BOUNDARY BLURRING

In some ways blurring boundaries between work and home may be beneficial. Communication technologies can allow for greater flexibility in managing work and non-work demands, as it gives employees greater control over when and where they can complete their work and may help employees to combine work and non-work responsibilities. For example, there would have been no possibility of parents managing to complete multiple responsibilities of working from home and attempting to educate school-aged children during the global pandemic without the presence of technology. Unquestionably, the boundaries between work and home life for such families were blurred more than ever before during this time, but technology made it possible for some elements of the world to continue, which would not have been the case 20–30 years prior.

NEGATIVE EFFECTS OF BOUNDARY BLURRING

However, other researchers suggest that the use of technology to work in previously 'personal time' means that time spent answering work emails and calls is time that cannot be devoted to care activities, household chores or interactions with family members. Derks et al. (2015) suggest that this 'subtle' way of extending work hours should be recognised because answering emails outside regular office hours seems harmless and therefore consequences (e.g., lack of psychological detachment and subsequent burnout) might go unnoticed. Indeed, others have found that behaviours such as keeping smartphones turned on during off-job time, glancing at them repeatedly, carrying them around all the time, and responding to emails in the evening can have a negative impact. Indeed, Yuan et al. (2018) found that these types of behaviours were positively associated with turnover intention, mediated by emotional exhaustion.

WHAT IMPACTS WHETHER 'BLURRING THE BOUNDARIES' IS DETRIMENTAL TO WELLBEING?

We've established that whether technology blurring the boundaries between time at work and time at home has a negative impact on wellbeing will largely depend on the individual employee's preferences and life circumstances, as well as the extent to which the employee feels pressurised by their employer to do so. For example, there is evidence that positive attitudes towards communication technologies in employees may predict decreased work–life conflict when work-related technology is used extensively outside regular work hours.

At the organisational level however, the following areas can impact on whether technology 'blurring boundaries' is an issue.

WHO PAYS FOR THE TECHNOLOGY

Equity theory (Adams, 1963) suggests that individuals are inclined to reciprocate investments from their organisation (e.g. the smartphone) with equal outcomes (e.g. work-related effort). As such, where the organisation has paid for a smartphone, the employee may feel obliged to reciprocate by being available on it during evenings and at weekends.

CLEAR EXPECTATIONS ABOUT AVAILABILITY

Increased connectivity with work via technology may contribute to stress and burnout when it is unclear when it is appropriate to contact employees via technology during their free time, and the amount and quality of work that is expected from them during these times. Some organisations set clear expectations about whether or not employees need to be 'online' outside office hours. For example, in 2012 Volkswagen took the decision to prevent servers from sending work emails to employees outside office hours. However, it appears that relatively few organisations have formal policies for helping workers cope with the stress of being almost perpetually connected to the workplace. Policy lagging behind practice is an area that work psychologists must navigate frequently when working with organisations around wellbeing.

SOCIAL NORMS IN THE WORKPLACE

Derks et al. (2015) identified supervisor and peer (other employees) norms or expectations as an influencing factor in the level of perceived work–home interference employees experience. Derks and colleagues define supervisor expectations as the urge to respond to messages during evening hours to 'measure up' to what employees believe are the expectations of their supervisor. In a similar vein, norms of colleagues are defined as the urge to respond to messages during evening hours because anyone else does and they want to be part of the group. Therefore if out-of-hours technology use is *not* the norm, it is less likely to impact on employees' WLB than if it is what is expected by others in the workplace.

WHOSE RESPONSIBILITY IS WELLBEING AT WORK?

So far in this chapter we've explored some of the causes and outcomes of wellbeing at work and work-related stress. Much of the research on these topics looks at what organisations can and should do relating to wellbeing, but even where an organisation that has taken significant measures to maximise wellbeing (for example, the physical workspace, processes, policies, benefits), there is an onus on individual employees to engage with these measures. As such, in order to achieve wellbeing at work, individuals must take responsibility for their own wellbeing in collaboration with their employer. There is also evidence that employees' peers can impact significantly on their wellbeing, for example support from colleagues at work being a mediating factor between workload and wellbeing (Aalto et al., 2018). Thus it could be argued that it is everyone's responsibility to look after their own – and to some extent – others' wellbeing.

Nonetheless, given that much of many people's lives is spent at work (especially given the 'always on' culture afforded by technology), there is increasingly an expectation from employees that the company they work for will provide opportunities for them to achieve wellbeing at work. For this to be effective, employee wellbeing needs to be part of a regular business dialogue and be deeply embedded into an organisational culture, rather than viewed and treated as a stand-alone consideration.

TYPES OF EMPLOYMENT

UNEMPLOYMENT

It would be forgivable to think of wellbeing in relation to work as an issue only for those individuals who are currently working. However, unemployment can have a significant negative impact on individual wellbeing, as summarised by Overell:

> The most potent lesson of the twentieth century regarding the nature of working life is that whilst work itself can be good or bad, the absence of work over a sustained period of time represents a serious threat to individual and social wellbeing.

(2009, p. 1)

Indeed, Warr (2007a) proposed that unemployed individuals experience significantly more negative feelings compared to those who are employed. However, the negative impacts of unemployment on wellbeing are not necessarily permanent, as some evidence suggests that when people return to employment, mental health improvements can outweigh any deteriorations associated with a job loss. This suggests that regaining employment may lead to better wellbeing than the person had experienced prior to becoming unemployed.

UNDEREMPLOYMENT

Underemployment can refer to three situations for the individual, and has been found to relate to lower objective (e.g. salary) and subjective (job satisfaction) career success as well as to poorer psychological and physical health.

OVER-QUALIFICATION

The education, skill levels or experience the individual has far exceed that which is required for the job role. For example, a recent graduate with a first-class psychology degree who is working as a cleaner might experience this type of underemployment.

INVOLUNTARY PART-TIME WORK

Employees who could (and would like to) be working full-time but can only find part-time work.

OVERSTAFFING

Also known as *hidden unemployment*, where businesses or entire economies employ workers who are not fully occupied – for example, workers currently not being used to produce goods or services due to legal or social restrictions or because the work is highly seasonal.

Following the global economic downturn in 2008/09 there was an increase in the percentage of the UK workforce that was identified as underemployed. Students graduating from university are one group likely to be particularly affected, as in recent years the number of people graduating from higher education globally has increased while the state of the economy has decreased the flexibility and demand in the labour market. As a result, the enduring economic crisis has resulted in a larger mismatch between supply and demand for graduates.

OVEREMPLOYMENT

Overemployment can be defined as working longer hours than one wants to. Importantly, note that it is not necessarily the number of hours that an individual is working that constitutes whether they are over-employed; rather it is whether or not the amount someone is working is greater than they want it to be. So, it is possible for someone working part-time to be overemployed, and someone working 55 hours a week not to be.

POSITIVE PSYCHOLOGY

Towards the beginning of this chapter, we looked at the CIPD definition of wellbeing, which fits with the approach of positive psychology in the workplace. Here we will explore this area in more detail. The positive psychology movement emerged from dissatisfaction with the development of psychology as a healing profession, whereby psychologists' roles were to 'make people better'. In their now seminal article, Seligman and Csikszentmihalyi (2000) summarised concisely the drivers for positive psychology:

> Psychologists ... have come to understand quite a bit about how people survive and endure under conditions of adversity. ... However, psychologists know very little about how normal people flourish under more benign conditions.

> *(2000, p. 8)*

ACTIVITY: REFLECT ON PSYCHOLOGISTS'
ROLES IN POSITIVE PSYCHOLOGY

What you have likely noticed throughout the course of this book is that a work psychologist's role is often to identify and solve problems. Indeed, an organisation becoming aware that something has gone wrong is often the point when work psychologists' support is sought. Now ask yourself the following questions:

- What if an organisation, a team or an employee is functioning without any obvious problems that need to be fixed? Does that automatically mean that an 'optimum state' has been achieved?
- Does that also mean, by extension, that there is no place for the expertise of work psychologists unless things are going badly?
- What if wellbeing at work was about more than simply trying to avoid work-related stress, burnout and work–life imbalance?
- What would this look like in practice?

These are some of the areas explored in this section.

Let's look again at the Chartered Institute of Personnel and Development's definition of wellbeing at work:

> Creating an environment to promote a state of contentment which allows an employee to flourish and achieve their full potential for the benefit of themselves and their organisation.
>
> *(CIPD, 2007, p. 21)*

Nowhere does this definition refer to avoiding illness, minimising stress or 'fixing' people who have been 'broken' by work, hence the introduction of positive psychology as a relevant field of study in relation to wellbeing. Sceptics of the philosophy of positive psychology argue that organisations are environments that place demands on employees that erode their capacity and energy. Thus, it could be argued that all work is inevitably and inherently wearing on employees, and therefore the focus *should* be on preventing and fixing damage (as it more traditionally has been), rather than on developing positive practices. However, the counter-argument to this position is that, because of the potential of work to erode employees' wellbeing, it becomes even more important to identify employees' strengths and maintain conditions in which strengths can be exercised to stimulate psychological growth.

The study of positive psychology in the workplace can be defined by looking at measurable human resource strengths and psychological capabilities. We will now look at two such resources and capacities often researched in positive psychology: psychological capital and mindfulness.

PSYCHOLOGICAL CAPITAL (PSYCAP)

More frequently known as PsyCap, this construct is the combination of several other characteristics, and is characterised as follows:

1. Having confidence to take on and put in the necessary effort to succeed at challenging tasks (*self-efficacy*)
2. Making a positive attribution about succeeding now and in the future (*optimism*)
3. Persevering towards goals and, when necessary, redirecting paths to goals in order to succeed (*hope*)
4. When beset by problems and adversity, sustaining and bouncing back and even beyond to attain success (*resilience*) (Luthans et al., 2007, p. 3).

PsyCap is considered to be a higher-order factor, which means its effects are greater than the sum of its parts when it comes to relationships with work-related outcomes. In other words, it shows greater associations with performance outcomes than its component parts do independently. It is possible that this effect occurs because PsyCap incorporates the coping mechanism(s) that the four individual components have in common.

Overwhelmingly, the literature suggests that PsyCap is beneficial to both organisations and employees in promoting desirable outcomes, with positive outcomes including moderating the role of job demands and stressors, increased job satisfaction, team organisational citizenship behaviours, employees' health and turnover intention. In a meta-analysis of the published and 'grey' literature available on PsyCap at the time, Avey et al. (2010) also identified that PsyCap alleviates undesirable outcomes such as employees' counterproductive behaviours.

Given the overwhelming evidence in the literature that PsyCap is positively related to desirable workplace outcomes, the next question for work psychologists is: How can we increase employees' levels of PsyCap? The answer to this largely depends on whether PsyCap is a 'trait' or a 'state'.

TABLE 4.3 Traits versus states

Traits	States
Longer lasting, enduring characteristics that are more stable across situations; more difficult to change	Temporary moods or behaviours that depend largely on the situation; open to development

Prior research on the constructs which together make up PsyCap (hope, resilience, optimism and efficacy) supports that they are developable both individually and when combined into a higher-order construct, which suggests that PsyCap is more state-like than trait-like.

ACTIVITY: REFLECT ON WHAT NEXT FOR PSYCAP

The literature to date suggests that PsyCap is a highly positive construct to develop within the workplace, with numerous positive work-related outcomes. However, compared to many other psychological constructs, PsyCap is in its infancy in terms of having a theory-driven conceptualisation and evidence base. As such, many questions about PsyCap remain unanswered, and PsyCap should certainly not be viewed as a panacea. Some key questions remain:

- What are the possible moderators of when PsyCap may be more or less important or useful in the workplace?
- What are the antecedents of PsyCap?
- Where exactly on the state–trait continuum does PsyCap sit?

- Which other constructs related to positive organisational behaviours does PsyCap include? And what does it not include?
- What are the longitudinal individual- and organisational-level outcomes of PsyCap?
- What are the psychometric properties of PsyCap, with a particular focus on test–retest reliability and within-subject variability?

MINDFULNESS

Unless you have been studiously avoiding both social media and anyone with a job, it has likely come to your attention that mindfulness has become hugely popular as a means of stress relief and as an antidote to the hectic pace of life many of us experience these days. In fact the word is thrown around so often that it is possible that as a population we may have lost sight of what it does and does not mean.

> Mindfulness begins by bringing awareness to current experience – observing and attending to the changing field of thoughts, feelings and sensations from moment to moment – by regulating the focus on attention. This leads to a feeling of being very alert in the here-and-now.
> *(Bishop et al., 2004)*

Mindfulness has its roots in the ancient Buddhist tradition of meditation, although its use and zeitgeist-like status in the Western world has deviated somewhat from this original practice (not least by removing the religious aspects). Over the past three decades mindfulness has gained significant popularity in medicine and clinical psychology, and researchers have frequently examined mindfulness meditation for its role in alleviating symptoms of physical and psychological disorders in clinical populations, and as a stress reduction technique in nonclinical populations (e.g. Kiken et al., 2017; Taylor et al., 2016). Note however that this use of mindfulness does not fit with the aims of positive psychology, which focuses on optimum functioning rather than reducing (di)stress.

Research into mindfulness in the workplace is truly in its infancy compared to other areas of research into wellbeing at work. In one of the earliest studies of mindfulness in the workplace, McCormick and Hunter (2008) analysed interviews with eight managers and professionals who have a meditation practice. They suggested that persons who practise mindfulness may experience a wealth of benefits, examples of which included:

- Being more likely to experience work difficulties as challenges than threats
- Being better able to cope and remain calm in difficult work situations
- Being more accepting of their work situation
- Enjoying their work more
- Being more adaptable at work
- Being less concerned with material acquisition and wealth
- Having more positive interpersonal relations at work

Being more likely to derive meaning in life from more sources than just work.

But while qualitative research provides rich and detailed data about a specific area, it cannot empirically establish cause and effect between variables. In other words, it is possible that these findings tell us more about the *type* of people who practise mindfulness at work than they tell us about the *benefits* (i.e. outcomes) of mindfulness. However, more recently experimental research designs have begun to emerge which have advocated the use of mindfulness as a way of increasing wellbeing and resilience and decreasing stress in student populations.

Dane (2011) noted that research and theory are underdeveloped with regard to whether and how mindfulness fosters or inhibits task performance in the workplace. Dane proposed a model to predict the impacts of mindfulness on work tasks. In summary, the model suggests:

> The relationship between mindfulness and task performance is *positive* when one operates in a dynamic task environment (environments in which individuals make a series of interdependent decisions in real time, such as the contexts of negotiations, emergency response operations and crisis management situations) *and* has a high level of task expertise.
>
> The relationship between mindfulness and task performance is *negative* when one operates in a static task environment (where relationships between aspects of the task are relatively stable and predictable) *and* is a task novice.

This model is supported by Taylor et al. (2016) who found that in a sample of primary school teachers, a mindfulness-based intervention reduced teacher stress through a variety of ways including increased emotional regulation and coping and increased efficacy for forgiveness and compassion. Given that teaching is uncertain and attentionally, socially and emotionally demanding work, and the sample had a mean of 15.2 years of teaching experience, this provides some support for Dane's model. However, much more research is needed in the workplace to draw any robust or generalisable conclusions about the benefits of mindfulness at work.

SUMMARY

In summary, research and practice relating to wellbeing at work are incredibly broad and span numerous associated topics including working conditions, work–life balance and work–home interaction, work-related stress, interventions and positive psychology. As work psychologists the key is to use evidence-based practice to increase wellbeing wherever possible – but to do this requires careful measurement of employees' wellbeing which we know to be challenging! For this reason, wellbeing is a topic than lends itself particularly well to qualitative and mixed-methods research designs, as it is people's experiences and the interaction between their environment and their individual differences which are key in designing interventions to maximise wellbeing at work.

RECOMMENDATIONS FOR FURTHER READING

Bliese, P., Edwards, J., and Sonnentag, S. (2017). Stress and well-being at work: A century of empirical trends reflecting theoretical and societal influences. *Journal of Applied Psychology, 102*(3), 389–402.

Chung, H., and Van der Lippe, T. (2020). Flexible working, work–life balance, and gender equality: Introduction. *Social Indicators Research, 151,* 365–381.

Dodge, R., Daly, A., Huyton, J., and Sanders, L. (2012). The challenge of defining wellbeing. *International Journal of Wellbeing, 2*(3), 222–235.

Rasool, S. F., Wang, M., Tang, M., Saeed, A., and Iqbal, J. (2021). How toxic workplace environment effects [*sic*] the employee engagement: The mediating role of organizational support and employee wellbeing. *International Journal of Environmental Research and Public Health, 18*(5), 2294.

5

WORK DESIGN, ORGANISATIONAL CHANGE AND DEVELOPMENT

In this chapter we introduce motivational aspects of work design and the nature of change in organisations (occasional or constant), as well as approaches to managing change. Systems theory of the impact of external factors on organisations in the 21st century is also introduced, as well as explorations of the concepts of organisational performance and effectiveness, culture versus climate, and different organisational structures.

Notably, ergonomics and human–machine interaction are an area of work design that historically fell into the domain of work psychologists. In more recent years, ergonomics has moved to the periphery of the profession and is now the domain of ergonomists (also known as human factors specialists) who focus on the safety and efficiency of equipment, systems and transportation. As such, ergonomics is not discussed in this chapter.

WORK DESIGN

Work design is a broad concept, because it acknowledges both the job (i.e., tasks and responsibilities) and its link with the broader environment (i.e., where and how people work). Interest in work design theories first came about in the mid-20th century and were focused on the prevalent demographics and work contexts of the time: male

DOI: 10.4324/9781315169880-5

shop floor workers in large-scale manufacturing environments. Both the working environment and the composition of the people working within it have changed dramatically since then. To give a few (non-exhaustive) examples, customer-facing work has increased significantly; as many manufacturing tasks have been taken over by technology, humans are now working increasingly at the 'front line' of customer service, rather than behind the scenes. Office for National Statistics data shows that in 2022 the workplace is no longer 'male dominated' with over 70% of women aged 16–64 now working outside the home. There has also been an increase in 'knowledge workers' – employees who apply theoretical and analytical knowledge, acquired through formal education, to developing new products and services. These include, for example, people working in product development, consultancy and information systems. Developments in technology have had – and continue to have – a huge impact on the way that work is conducted, enabling many workers to work away from designated 'office' sites and, in some cases, work anywhere in the world. In the same vein, teams can now be virtual, meaning people who work together may be distributed globally and across different time zones. After the global pandemic in 2020 forced many organisations to adapt to remote working (working in locations other than the organisation's premises – in this instance, predominantly at home), this has become the norm more than ever before.

Whereas once it was considered normal for employees to spend their entire working career with one or two companies, the increased entrepreneurial mindset in younger generations alongside factors such as organisational downsizing and a less stable economy means that notions of a 'typical career' are changing; people now expect to move between organisations much more often than ever before. Likewise, the labour market is being increasingly characterised by the 'gig economy', whereby people choose to work in short-term contracts and/or freelance, instead of choosing permanent jobs.

It is interesting, given the rate and extent of change in how people work both as individuals and with others, that since a peak in the 1980s there has been a relative dearth of research into work design – perhaps due to the success of the job characteristics model (see below) leading researchers to think the case was closed (Humphrey et al., 2007). But as the world of work changes at an ever-increasing pace, there is undeniably scope to examine how the new compositions of the work environment and workforce impact on what 'good' work design looks like.

In the following sections we will introduce early theories of job and work design and outline how these have been extended in line with more recent changes in the workplace.

THE TWO-FACTOR THEORY OF JOB DESIGN

Herzberg et al. (1959) offered the first theory relating to designing individual jobs. Their two-factor theory identified 'motivators', intrinsic to the work itself (e.g., the level of interest in the tasks), and 'hygiene factors', extrinsic to the work (e.g. work conditions) as the key factors of job design. Herzberg and colleagues proposed that motivators affected satisfaction and had little impact on dissatisfaction, whereas the opposite was true for hygiene factors. This theory remained highly influential for a decade, but eventually lost support as evidence repeatedly failed to confirm this. The theory did however encourage the idea of motivation and job enrichment – the latter referring to building scope for personal achievement and recognition alongside more challenging work through opportunities for both personal growth and career advancement.

JOB CHARACTERISTICS MODEL (JCM)

Advancing Herzberg et al.'s earlier work, Hackman and Oldham (1976) suggested that five work characteristics make jobs more satisfying for workers:

- Autonomy: the freedom an individual has to carry out their work
- Skill variety: how much an individual must use different skills to perform their job
- Task identity: the extent to which an individual can complete an entire piece of work
- Task significance: how much a job impacts others' lives

Feedback from the job: the extent to which a job itself imparts information about an individual's performance (as opposed to other people providing that feedback).

Hackman and Oldham asserted that these work characteristics increased positive behavioural (e.g., job performance) and attitudinal (e.g., job satisfaction) outcomes, and decreased negative behavioural outcomes (e.g., absenteeism). The model received a wealth of support in the literature but has some notable gaps. The JCM focuses on a limited set of motivational work features which, while important, ignore other salient aspects of work such as the social environment and work context (Humphrey et al., 2007). However, research in other areas has documented the importance of both the social environment and work context for a wide range of outcomes (see Chapters 4 and 6).

BEYOND THE JCM

To extend research into work design beyond the JCM, other scholars have proposed a variety of additional variables that are important to consider in this context, and in the changing world of work. Some of these taxonomies are outlined below.

Task characteristics have been the most commonly investigated areas of motivational work design. They are primarily concerned with how the work itself is accomplished and the range and nature of tasks associated with a particular job and were the original focus of the JCM.

Initially viewed as the amount of freedom and independence people have to carry out their work assignment, more recent research has suggested that the task characteristic of autonomy reflects the extent to which a job allows freedom, independence, work scheduling discretion, decision-making, and choosing how to perform tasks. Thus, autonomy is generally agreed to include three interrelated aspects centred on self-determination in (a) work scheduling, (b) decision-making, and (c) work methods (Morgeson and Humphrey, 2006).

Knowledge characteristics reflect the kinds of knowledge, skill and ability demands that are placed on individuals as a result of their job. By distinguishing task and knowledge characteristics, researchers acknowledged that jobs can be (re)designed to increase the task demands, knowledge demands or both. These include:

- *Job complexity*: The extent to which the tasks on a job are complex and difficult to perform. A degree of difficulty is considered to be positively motivational because work that involves complex tasks requires the use of numerous high-level skills and is more mentally demanding and challenging.

- *Information processing*: The degree to which a job requires attending to and processing data or other information.
- *Problem solving*: This reflects how much a job requires unique ideas or solutions. It reflects the more active cognitive processing requirements of a job, such as generating unique or innovative ideas or solutions, diagnosing and solving non-routine problems, and preventing or recovering from errors.
- *Specialisation*: The extent to which the job involves performing specialised tasks or requires the person to have specialised skills and knowledge. Unlike the breadth of activities and skills involved in a job, specialisation is about the depth of knowledge and skill in a particular area.

Social characteristics are the elements of the job that relate to individuals' interactions with others. These are thought to include:

- *Social support*: This is the extent of opportunities for advice and assistance from others. Although not traditionally studied in job design contexts, research from other domains suggests that social support is critical for wellbeing (see Chapter 4). This is particularly true for jobs that are stressful or lack many motivational work characteristics.
- *Interdependence*: The degree to which the job depends on others, and others depend on it, to complete aspects of work – i.e. the 'connectedness' of jobs to each other. Kiggundu (1981) argued that there are two distinct forms of interdependence (a) the extent to which work flows from one job to other jobs (initiated interdependence) and (b) the extent to which a job is affected by work from other jobs (received interdependence).
- *Interaction outside the organisation*: The extent to which the job requires employees to interact and communicate with individuals outside the organisation, such as suppliers, customers, etc.
- *Feedback from others*: How much others in the organisation provide information about performance. Note this is distinct from feedback in the JCM because this is feedback from colleagues, not from the job itself.

Contextual characteristics relate to the physical environment in which the job takes place. These are thought to include:

- *Ergonomics*: The degree to which a job allows correct or appropriate posture and movement. While literature on this topic one was very much focused on manufacturing environments, nowadays there is an increasing focus on human–computer interaction as technology-based roles dominate the workforce (Boy, 2017).
- *Physical demands*: The physical strength, endurance, effort and activity aspects of the job.
- *Work conditions*: The environment within which a job is performed. It includes the presence of health hazards, noise, temperature and cleanliness of the working environment.
- *Equipment use*: The variety and complexity of the technology and equipment used in a job.

JOB DESIGN FOR EMPLOYEE HAPPINESS

While it is widely acknowledged that job design will have an influence on employees' satisfaction and engagement, this is often with a view to the subsequent implications on the productivity and quality of work output. In other words, personal or social outcomes of job design have focused most often on how they relate to organisational gain. Indeed, in terms of consequences, there is now considerable evidence that variations in happiness have a causal impact on a range of day-to-day activities, for example high or low job performance, staff turnover, absenteeism, citizenship behaviour and so on. However, research is also emerging which looks at employee happiness as an important, stand-alone outcome.

Warr (2007b) argues that traditional models of job design omit many of the elements that relate to employee happiness. He suggests other important elements include factors such as valued social position, opportunity for skill use and acquisition (a setting's potential for applying and developing expertise and knowledge) and opportunity to receive income at a certain level.

However, Warr also notes the non-linear nature of associations between happiness and job characteristics; for example, happiness does not continue to increase at the same rate with more and more of a job characteristic. There is also the consideration that different people have different baselines of happiness (i.e., some people are more 'naturally happy' than others) and so job design can only influence an individual's overall happiness to an extent.

Nonetheless, Dutschke and colleagues (2019) proposed that happiness relating to job design depends on five dimensions: self-fulfilment, attaining goals, (support and inspiration from) leadership, sustainability and job/family balance, and group and organisational work.

JOB CRAFTING

Some research suggests that job designs are simply starting points, from which employees can introduce changes and redefine their roles in personally meaningful ways, known as job crafting. This is where employees independently modify aspects of their jobs to improve the fit between the characteristics of the job and their own needs, abilities and preferences. A core feature of job crafting is that employees initiate and carry out alterations in their jobs from the bottom up, rather than managers directing changes from the top down like many job redesign interventions. This enables employees to use the unique knowledge they have of their jobs and themselves to craft their jobs in ways that feel better suited to their own preferences.

Rudolph and colleagues (2017) propose that this can be done in four key ways (these relate to the job demand resources model – see Chapter 4):

- Increasing challenging job demands – e.g., seeking out new tasks and responsibilities aligned to their interests
- Decreasing hindering job demands – e.g., finding additional resources to meet stressful demands
- Increasing structural job resources – e.g., seeking greater autonomy in their role
- Increasing social job resources – e.g., making time to meet with colleagues/leaders they deem to be inspiring.

Numerous studies have found that job crafting is related to higher work engagement and job satisfaction, as employees have shaped their job to meet their own preferences and needs.

In summary, there are a great many factors of work design that can impact on individuals' motivation and engagement in their roles, and accordingly there is a wealth of research to support many of these. However, as political climates, workforce compositions and ways of working change, so too do the factors influencing motivation at work, and research has some catching up to do to address these issues in the contemporary workplace. We will now look at how change happens within organisations and ways of managing this which should also be considered in any research or practice relating to work design.

ORGANISATIONAL CHANGE

Organisational change has been defined in numerous ways, but for the purpose of this chapter, we'll use Martins' (2011, p. 692) definition:

> The study and practice of creating or responding to differences in the states of individuals, groups, organisations and collectives over time ... for example an individual changing from one role to another, a group changing from one decision process to another, or an organisation going from one structural arrangement to another.

DISCONTINUOUS/PLANNED VERSUS CONTINUOUS CHANGE

Attitudes towards organisational change in both the literature and practice have been evolving over the last few decades. Early approaches suggested that organisations could not be effective or improve performance if they were constantly changing, because employees need routines in order to be effective and improve job performance. In this approach, change was considered to be an occasional or 'discontinuous', top-down activity which is planned in advance, and led by leaders and managers in a business.

A seminal model of discontinuous change is Lewin's (1947) three-step model, which proposed that, before change and new behaviour can be successfully adopted, the previous behaviour has to be discarded. This model is well known and is still used by many organisations today.

Step 1: Unfreezing. Lewin proposed that humans are generally in a state of equilibrium achieved by a complex combination of driving and restraining forces (which support and resist change, respectively). He argued that the equilibrium needs to be destabilised (unfrozen) before old behaviours can be unlearned and new behaviour successfully adopted. Lewin suggested that this unfreezing would be different across different situations and requires people to feel confident that they will be protected from loss or other negative consequences before they are able to accept the new way of working and reject old behaviours.

Step 2: Moving. In this stage, people move to the new equilibrium. The outcome of this can vary hugely due to the different forces acting upon them.

Step 3: Refreezing. This is re-entering a state of equilibrium that is in line with all of the individual's other behaviours. For this reason, Lewin saw successful change as a group activity because, unless group norms and routines are also transformed, changes to individual behaviour will not be sustained. In organisational terms, refreezing often requires changes to organisational culture, norms, policies and practices.

Before long, Lewin's (1947) model was being criticised for being too group-based, consensual (i.e. everyone has to agree to the planned change before it happens) and relatively slow in nature compared to the reality for organisations operating in an ever-changing world. The planned/discontinuous model of change was thought to focus mostly on small-scale and incremental change and therefore has been criticised for being less applicable to situations that require rapid and transformational change. Perhaps a more important criticism in today's world of work is that the planned approach is based on the assumptions that organisations operate under constant conditions, and that they can move in a pre-planned manner from one stable state to another (Bamford and Forrester, 2003). But the pace of change in businesses has never been faster, nor come in so many different forms (Burnes, 2004a). Events such as the influx of younger generations (Generations Y and Z) entering the workforce with very different expectations about work than their predecessors, the global economic downturn in 2008, and more recently global events such as the Covid-19 pandemic have required organisations globally to adapt and respond in ways that clearly demonstrate the impact of external forces on an organisation.

Many researchers and practitioners now argue that change is an ever-present part of organisational life and inseparable from organisational strategy (e.g. Burnes, 2004b). This approach suggests that change is so rapid it is impossible for organisational leaders to effectively identify, plan and implement the necessary organisational responses. As a result, the responsibility for organisational change has to become increasingly the shared responsibility of everyone within an organisation – not just those at the top.

In line with this viewpoint is the *continuous transformation model*, which argues that in order to survive organisations must develop the ability to fundamentally change themselves *continuously*. This is particularly the case in the fast-moving sectors such as retail and computers where new trends and technology appear almost daily, although there is a general consensus in the literature that change comes in all shapes and size and therefore affects organisations in all industries (Todnem By, 2005). Thinking once more about the impact of Covid-19 on organisations, there have likely been very few organisations (if any) across all industries that did not have to make some adjustments to accommodate the changes happening globally.

SYSTEMS THEORY OF ORGANISATIONS

So far in this chapter, we have briefly made reference to the external and internal influences on organisations that prompt them to change. It is important to note that organisations do not exist in isolation – they are likely to be affected to a greater or lesser extent by the political and economic landscape they are operating in. One way of conceptualising the relationship between an organisation, its component parts (i.e., the groups of people who work within it) and its environment is *systems theory*, which was adapted for use in the organisational setting by Katz and Khan (1966). This approach conceptualises the organisation as an organism, with its component parts all interacting with, and interrelated to, each other. The organisation likely also has subsystems within it such as departments and teams, that have their own specific functions and responsibilities which interact with each other – the number and complexity of these will depend on the size of the organisation and how established it is. Because all parts of the organisation are thought to be interconnected, the theory follows that all subsystems in an organisation are affected if changes are made to any one subsystem.

Other key assumptions of systems theory include that the organisation is an *open system* which both impacts and is impacted by the environment it operates in – meaning organisations are constantly adapting and changing. This suggests that for organisations to be effective, they must be aware of what is occurring in their current environment and adjust themselves accordingly in order to remain successful.

SYSTEMS THEORY AND BREXIT: AN EXAMPLE

We will use the UK's decision to leave the European Union ('Brexit'), and one of the UK's 'Big Four' accounting firms as an example of systems theory in practice. Consider the impact that Brexit continues to have on how the organisation operates within the UK, and the potential impact of the 'Big Four' organisation on the political climate in the UK. For example, if influential leaders in the organisation are known to be close to those in power in the UK government, they may have had some input into negotiations on the terms of Britain leaving the European Union. An example of this may be that if the leaders could have made government officials aware that if certain terms were not agreed during Brexit, it may limit the organisation's ability to grow within the UK, and therefore impact on the number of jobs and revenue created, and subsequently tax paid by that organisation to the government. Given the size of the 'Big Four' organisations and the number of employees they have, this could have significant negative outcomes for the UK government.

Thinking about the possible impact of Brexit within the organisation and between its component parts, the effect of the UK's exit from the European Union on the strength of the pound will impact on many areas, including the business' financial worth in the global economy. This in turn could impact and be impacted by numerous other areas – a few examples are given in Figure 5.1, but you may be able to think of many more.

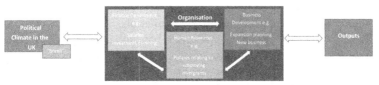

FIGURE 5.1 An example of systems theory for a 'Big Four' organisation and Brexit

CHANGE MANAGEMENT

Now that we have defined organisational change and considered the perspectives on the extent to which change is a constant, we will consider how change can be managed in organisations. Change management has been defined as 'the process of continually renewing an organisation's direction, structure, and capabilities to serve the ever-changing needs of external and internal customers' (Moran and Brightman, 2001, p. 111) and is notorious among researchers and practitioners alike for being one of the most challenging managerial activities because it requires redefining organisational and individuals' goals, anticipating needs of internal and external customers, and adapting either reactively or, preferably, proactively to them.

If we take the position that change is a constant in organisations then change management becomes embedded in everyday organisational life, rather than being a stand-alone activity. As such, it is of vital importance to an organisation's success that employees are able to continually monitor and adapt to changing environments, and that managers are able to take employees with them on the journey of change. Therefore, the challenge for organisations is not only to manage the change process, but also to create a climate in which employees embrace change.

However, Pieterse and colleagues (2012) report that approximately 70% of all change initiatives fail (i.e., do not meet their desired objectives of moving an organisation from one position to another), leading to disappointed expectations and enormous costs in terms of time and resources. Similarly, according to research from the Chartered Institute of Personnel and Development, fewer than 60% of re-organisations meet their stated objectives, usually bottom-line (financial) improvement. Why is this the case? Edmonds (2011) suggests that, because no two organisations are the same, it is impossible to create a template for change that meets every organisation's needs, so there is likely to be an element of organisations needing to work out what to do while the change process is happening. However, Burnes (2004b) did suggest some key strategic (high-level) steps to follow when managing change that could provide a starting point for organisations to follow.

BURNES' (2004B) STRATEGIC APPROACH TO CHANGE MANAGEMENT

1. Create a vision: the organisation's vision needs to be created and communicated in consultation with employees in order to gain their commitment.

2. Develop strategies: strategies need to be developed for each of the functions (such as marketing, personnel, finance and product development). These form part of the overall strategic plan and can be viewed as linking the current state of the organisation to its future.

3. Create the conditions for successful change: involves managers creating readiness for change amongst employees, thus reducing the likelihood of resistance to changes. This might be achieved through: making people aware of the pressures for change; giving regular feedback on performance; publicising successful change; understanding people's fears and concerns; encouraging communication; and involving those who are affected

4. Create the right culture: this will encourage, for example, flexibility, autonomy and group working. Where the existing culture is not conducive to change, a new culture is needed (see the next section on organisational culture in this chapter).

5. Assess the need for and type of change: an assessment of the need for change should precede the adoption of any change programme. Organisational change should be considered if: (a) the strategy highlights the need for change or improved performance; (b) current performance indicates severe problems or concerns; or (c) opportunities arise which offer significant improvements. The assessment should include not only a diagnosis of the problem, but also propose a range of possible solutions.

6. Plan and implement change: this should involve the planning and scheduling of the change programme, including the identification of key individuals and groups whose commitment is required to secure the changes.

7. Involvement: gaining the commitment and support of all those involved and affected by the change programme, so that these people can take some ownership of the change process.

8. Sustain the momentum: as the programme is implemented, commitment and enthusiasm can begin to wane, slowing progress

towards the programme's objectives. Managers must ensure that momentum is maintained through the provision of additional resources, supporting change agents, facilitating the development of new skills and the support of new behaviours through financial reward, praise or recognition.

9. Continuous improvement: once a change programme has been implemented, managers should be aware that continuous and gradual change should be ongoing in order to maintain competitive edge. Thus, companies should commit to continuous improvement, even after the completion of the change programme.

Now re-read Burnes' suggested approach, considering how long it would take to do each of these steps in practice. Taking point number 1 'Create a vision' as an example, how might this be achieved? In likelihood the answer is by analysing the organisation's position in the marketplace, gathering all Director-level employees and above to agree on the strategic direction of the company, seek input from employees at all levels, and numerous other activities. This alone could take months to achieve and huge amounts of resource and cost (think of the price of all the most senior people in an organisation meeting to discuss the vision from the viewpoint of their salaries alone, let alone costs from lost operational productivity). From this, we can see that the reality of managing change is that it is costly and complex.

OUTCOMES OF CHANGE

The way in which change is managed is a contentious issue as many practitioners and researchers alike suggest that theories and approaches to change management currently available to academics and practitioners are often contradictory, and lack empirical evidence (Todnem By, 2005). Indeed, the poor success rate of organisational change initiatives may be in part due to a lack of valid frameworks of how to implement and manage organisational change.

There is also a dearth of literature defining what successful change looks like, or the outcomes of a successful change initiative. As a result, it can be challenging for practitioners to evaluate whether a change initiative has been successful with no framework to benchmark against. Of course, each organisation will (or should) have its own goals that it is intending to reach through change, but unless these are clearly defined in measurable terms, it is challenging – if not impossible – to objectively assess the success of change management.

That said, there is some research on the role of managers and leaders in change processes, which will be covered in the next section.

THE ROLE OF MANAGERS AND LEADERS IN ORGANISATIONAL CHANGE

As we will discuss in Chapter 6, many academics and practitioners distinguish between managers and leaders in the workplace, and the same is also true when applied to organisational change. Stoughton and Ludema (2012) define leaders as the people who provide a framework for change by communicating their commitment to it, while managers adopt the new ways of thinking and behaving to turn the organisation's vision into change for action. Therefore, the distinction is *creating* the vision (leadership) versus *acting* on the vision (management). Arguably both are needed to ensure that people are engaged and committed to change, in order to embed it into an organisation.

One area where leaders have been found to be most instrumental in the success (however that may be defined) or otherwise of change, is in their ability to take employees with them through the change process, so that they remain committed to the organisation and their jobs and are content (or better, engaged and motivated) at work. Research has identified factors such as communication with employees, encouraging employee participation in the change and strength of supervisor–employee relationship as important in doing so. In the following sections we'll explore this in more detail.

RESISTANCE TO ORGANISATIONAL CHANGE

So far in this chapter, we have established that the successful management of change is essential if organisations are to survive and succeed in dynamic and unpredictable environments such as the one we live and work in today. One key variable that can prevent this from happening is employee resistance to organisational change; indeed, many researchers suggest that (poor) management of employee resistance is one of the main causes of unsuccessful change. Resistance has been defined as 'employee behaviour that seeks to challenge, disrupt or invert prevailing assumptions, discourses and power relations' (Collinson, 1994, p. 28).

Until fairly recently, this area was relatively unresearched at the individual level. However, Fugate et al. (2012) argue that employees are critically important to the success of change initiatives because they are either the change implementers or change recipients, and therefore their commitment to a large extent determines the ultimate success of the change process. As a result, getting employees to 'buy into' the change process and want it to be a success is key. However, Piderit (2000) warned that the label of 'resistance' can be used by organisations to dismiss potentially valid employee concerns about proposed changes, as managers in charge of rolling out change initiatives may blame others for failures rather than accepting their own role in it. As such, the considerations below remain intrinsically linked to the role of leaders and managers in the change process. Let's now look at two factors, in addition to management and leadership, which can impact on this. It is notable that most research on organisational change has looked at macro or systems levels, rather than taking a person-orientated focus.

PERCEIVED ORGANISATIONAL JUSTICE

Perceived organisational justice is the extent to which employees feel that interactions, procedures and outcomes in the workplace are fair (Baldwin, 2006). Research suggests that when employees perceive that there is organisational justice (i.e., that they are being treated fairly throughout a change process) they are likely to develop attitudes and behaviours that support successful implementation of change (Cobb et al., 1995). They are also more likely to demonstrate more positive attitudes and behaviours towards the organisation (Bernerth et al., 2007), with allied feelings of engagement in their work. Similarly, perceived organisational justice is generally predictive of higher levels of openness to and acceptance of change, cooperation with change and satisfaction with change. In practice what this means is that when employees are required to make changes to their day-to-day working lives, they need to see an equal benefit to themselves to consider it fair. If employees feel that their organisation is asking more from them than they are receiving in return, the change process may cause resistance and be less likely to be successful as a result.

PERSONAL ATTRIBUTES

A number of studies have found that employees' openness towards organisational change can be predicted by traits such as self-esteem, self-efficacy, risk tolerance, need for achievement and locus of control (the extent to which an individual believes themselves to be able to affect what happens around and to them). Such findings indicate that employees who are confident about their abilities to navigate change experience higher levels of readiness to change (Vakola, 2014) than those who do not. Such attributes can be assessed at the point of selection into the organisation or may be a focus for employee development programmes.

ORGANISATIONAL EFFECTIVENESS AND PERFORMANCE

If you were to ask any leaders in an organisation what the purpose of effective work design is, or why they want their organisation to change, they would most likely say to make the organisation more effective and to perform better. But what effectiveness and performance actually mean is a surprisingly hazy area, with very little consistency across the academic literature and/or practice. For example, in their review of 213 papers on organisational performance Richard et al. (2009) identified 207 different measures of organisational performance, and there is no universal agreement on how the performance of organisations ought to be measured, or at what level (e.g., individual, team or organisational).

There has also been a lack of clarity between organisational performance and organisational effectiveness, although Richard et al. (2009) separate these out as two distinct constructs.

Organisational performance encompasses three specific areas of firm outcomes:

- Financial performance (profits, return on assets, return on investment, etc.)
- Product market performance (sales, market share, etc.)
- Shareholder return (total shareholder return, economic value added, etc.).

Organisational effectiveness is broader and captures both organisational performance and the many internal performance outcomes normally associated with more efficient or effective operations. It also relates to external measures and considerations that are broader than organisational economics, such as corporate social responsibility.

For work psychologists, it's important to identify which of the areas of organisational effectiveness are of the greatest importance to the organisation, before designing and implementing a process to reach that end goal.

One way of increasing organisational *performance* is to ensure that the people selected into the roles are the best fit for that job, thus increasing the likelihood of them performing well in that role. See Chapter 2 for an overview of job analysis which is an important step in ensuring that the aspects of the role are understood in order to be able to identify a person specification to meet the requirements of the role and select the person(s) who best fit that specification.

ORGANISATIONAL CLIMATE AND CULTURE

Another widely discussed pair of terms in the organisational development and change literature is that of climate and culture. Although the two terms have frequently been used interchangeably and the constructs share similarities, organisational climate and culture are now generally accepted to be distinct things. French and Bell (1995) suggest that organisational *climate* is about how people react to policies and procedures, which is fairly easy to change. Organisational *culture*, however, is proposed to be the values, norms, beliefs and customs that individuals within a social group (i.e., the organisation) have in common. Culture guides beliefs on what is right and wrong and is much more difficult to change.

As climate is more about behaviours, and culture is more about the beliefs underlying them, these two distinct constructs tend to be measured differently, with most climate research using quantitatively based questionnaire measures which are applied across numerous organisations, while most culture researchers have advocated the use of qualitative measures and focus on each organisation individually.

Culture is considered to be a highly complex phenomenon, with what is observable only a small proportion of the overall construct. The metaphor of an iceberg can be used to imagine the layers of organisational culture (Hermans, 1970), whereby visible above the water are features of the organisation such as goals, technology, polices and procedures, services/products and so on. Under the water however is the rest of the cultural iceberg which cannot be seen, but actually forms the majority of the culture. These unseen elements can include how things 'really get done', informal interactions, group norms, and beliefs or assumptions of employees.

Similarly, Schein (1985) identified three levels of the cultural phenomenon in organisations, as follows.

ARTEFACTS

On the surface are the overt behaviours and other physical manifestations. This category includes:

- The physical layout
- The dress code
- The manner in which people address each other
- Company records
- Products
- Statements of philosophy
- Annual reports.

VALUES

Values are a sense of what ought to be. These are the values, norms, ideologies, charters and philosophies inherent in the organisation.

BASIC ASSUMPTIONS

At the deepest level are those things that are taken for granted as 'correct' ways of coping with the environment (basic assumptions). These are the underlying and usually unconscious assumptions that determine perceptions, thought processes, feelings and behaviour within an organisation.

ORGANISATIONAL STRUCTURES

Closely related to organisational culture is structure, which is formed by the way in which people are organised and their lines of communication. Structures usually emerge out of needing to group people together to get work done, although in some instances planned changes to organisational structures can occur.

Robbins and Judge (2017) suggest that there are six dimensions of organisations which vary to generate their structure. These include:

- *Specialisation*: How specialised the role is (i.e., are the tasks/knowledge required in the role very narrow or more varied?)
- *Departmentalisation*: How employees are grouped (e.g., by similarity of role or in multidisciplinary project teams)
- *Span of control*: The employee:manager ratio
- *Formalisation*: How formalised the way in which tasks are completed is
- *Chain of command*: The level of hierarchy in the reporting structures
- *Centralisation*: Who makes the important decisions (e.g., a small, centralised group of stakeholders, or the wider organisation together (decentralisation)).

FLAT STRUCTURES

Smaller organisations often have 'flat' structures which tend to have low formalisation of tasks, highly centralised decision-making approaches (e.g., by the founders only) and a wide span of control. This means that there are few levels of management and employees are supervised but also more involved in the decision-making processes as they are 'closer' to those making the decisions. However, as organisations grow, this approach to structuring an organisation can become unruly, and increased formalisation, departmentalisation and so on are often required to manage increasing numbers of employees effectively.

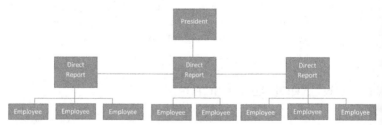

FIGURE 5.2 A flat organisational structure

TABLE 5.1 Pros and cons of flat organisational structures

Pros of flat structures	Cons of flat structures
Reduce time required to make decisions/solve problems by removing hierarchical sign-off	Employees may lack a specific person to report to, which creates confusion
Thought to increase communication and cooperation between employees	Typically produce generalists rather than specialists
Can reduce staff costs by having fewer levels of middle management	Specific job/role functions can be unclear
Can be beneficial for small organisations	Less suited to large organisations

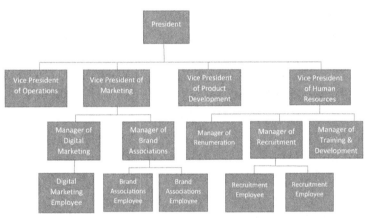

FIGURE 5.3 A functional organisational structure

FUNCTIONAL STRUCTURES

In functional organisational structures, employees are grouped by their function, which will differ by organisation. This approach is common in many organisations and is a somewhat 'common sense' approach to organisational structure because people who deal with the same sorts of tasks are grouped together in a hierarchical structure.

MATRIX STRUCTURES

Appearing in the 1970s and becoming increasingly popular ever since, matrix structures are where organisations are set up so that employees

TABLE 5.2 Pros and cons of functional organisational structures

Pros of functional structures	Cons of functional structures
Logical way of grouping activities within an organisation	Can promote 'siloed' working where information flow between departments/functions is limited
Allows development of specialised knowledge and skills	Managers are less 'well rounded' in terms of knowledge of functions
Easier for managers to deal with people whose work they share knowledge about	Generates specialists* rather than generalists

* Note this is listed as both a pro and a con – it can be either, depending on how the person wishes to shape their career and what the organisation requires from their senior management.

have two managers, usually in different departments, to report to. One is often a functional or subject matter expert manager, while the other is usually a line manager. This can be desirable when there is a need to share resources across an organisation and there are high levels of information processing (Tatum, 1981). This type of organisational structure is hierarchical.

Taking Figure 5.4 as an example, Engineer 1 may report both to the Vice President (e.g., for line managerial purposes such as holiday entitlement, appraisals and so on) and to Subject Matter Expert 1 regarding a specific project. In matrix structures it is also possible for employees of the same level to report to each other (e.g. Engineer 1 may report to Engineer 2 or vice versa) and for reporting to be inverse to position within the business (e.g. Subject Matter Expert 2 could report to Engineer 1 on a specific project).

Some researchers suggest that organisational structures shouldn't be static due to the fact that they are operating in a dynamic environment where most variables (technology, political climate, the people managing the organisation, etc) are constantly in flux – see systems theory. In reality, organisational structures often evolve somewhat haphazardly over time as the organisation grows or changes, and the environment it operates in does the same.

ORGANIC VERSUS MECHANISTIC STRUCTURES

Organic and mechanistic structures are considered to be opposite ends of a continuum, which ranges from flexibility to rigidity, and are a

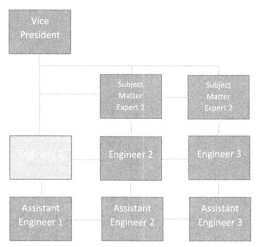

FIGURE 5.4 A matrix organisational structure

TABLE 5.3 Pros and cons of matrix organisational structures

Pros of matrix structures	Cons of matrix structures
Expertise and knowledge are shared more widely across people and projects than in a 1:1 employee:manager reporting system	Potential for confusion and conflict between different managers' roles and approaches
Increased communication and flexibility while retaining accountability	Multiple authorities can create confusion for reportees, so this structure requires people to be comfortable with ambiguity
Used to decentralise decision-making to improve competitive advantage (i.e., being able to respond quicker)	May over-emphasise group decision-making as there are so many possible reporting structures

higher-level characterisation of organisational structure than those outlined above. This concept is represented in the figure below.

Researchers have typically agreed that which organisational structure is 'better' (more suitable for a given organisation) depends on both the tasks the organisation conducts and the environment it is within. Evidence suggests that organic structures improve organisational performance when the tasks are non-routine, and the environment is uncertain,

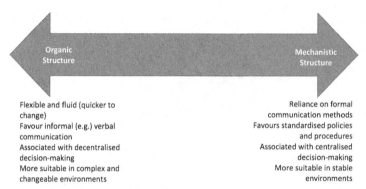

Flexible and fluid (quicker to change)
Favour informal (e.g.) verbal communication
Associated with decentralised decision-making
More suitable in complex and changeable environments

Reliance on formal communication methods
Favours standardised policies and procedures
Associated with centralised decision-making
More suitable in stable environments

FIGURE 5.5 Organic versus mechanistic structures

while mechanistic structures are better for organisational performance when the tasks are routine and the environment is certain. Bringing this research into the present day, researchers have found that organic structures are more suitable for organisations working with technological innovation because this is typically highly uncertain and non-routine (e.g., Hatum and Pettigrew, 2006). As the vast majority of organisations – both small and large – focus increasingly on technology as a way to reduce costs, reach a greater number of customers and thus increase revenue, there may be an argument that the days for mechanistic organisational structures contributing to organisational performance are numbered.

ACTIVITY

Place each of the structures on pages 000—000 where you think they sit on the organic to mechanistic continuum.

ORGANISATIONAL AGILITY

Organisational agility has been defined as the rapid and proactive adaptation of organisational elements to uncertain and unexpected changes. Two features of agility have been proposed in the literature:

- Responding to dynamics and threats in the best possible way and in the shortest possible time
- Identifying and capitalising on opportunities in the most effective and timely manner.

Organisational and workforce agility has been suggested to be important to the growth of businesses in competitive markets that face continuous and unanticipated change (Alavi et al., 2014) – such as today's global and volatile market. Indeed, organisations are realising that they must continually respond to their changeable and competitive environments to survive (Muduli, 2015). They are under pressure from customers to be more flexible, to deliver goods and services in a shorter time, and to offer a range of products and services – all at low costs and in line with ever-changing consumer requirements.

As agility in a workforce means that employees can react and adapt to change quickly and appropriately and can take advantage of such changes to benefit the organisation (Chonko and Jones, 2005), there is an ever-increasing need for organisations to increase their agility for competitive advantage.

However, limited research has sought to answer the question of how agility in a workforce can be increased. Where studies do exist, their context is almost exclusively in manufacturing and information technology-based industries. Nonetheless, some research suggests that factors relating to organisational structure have synergies with workforce and organisational agility. These include having virtual teams, employee involvement in management practices (e.g., 'power sharing' such as systems to create suggestions, self-management teams), decentralisation of decision-making and a flat structure (Alavi et al., 2014). In other words, organic structures appear to promote organisational agility more readily than mechanistic structures.

Today more than ever before, organisations are operating in turbulent economic and political environments, meaning that they need to adapt rapidly not only to remain competitive or relevant, but to survive. In this chapter we have looked at how work and jobs can be designed for optimum efficiency and employee happiness, and the many complex variables that feed into this. Work psychologists should apply this knowledge to empower organisations to evaluate their job designs and ways of working in line with the possibilities of the 21st century (e.g., incorporating elements of remote working, job crafting and other positive job characteristics) where practicable, to maximise not only employee output but their wellbeing and happiness too. Organisational change has also been discussed, with the general consensus among researchers and practitioners now being that the only constant is change. Ways of managing this and the importance of engaging employees with change journeys and making change feel equitable were outlined. Here, work psychologists can support managers and leaders in organisations to not only set and communicate strategic directions for an organisation, but also to ensure that employees 'buy into' the change and are able to understand the benefits for them in their own working lives, as well as to the organisation as a whole. Finally, this chapter looked at the relative pros and cons of different organisational structures. Matrix structures are fashionable at the moment and have many benefits, however as with anything in the field of work psychology, there is not a 'one size fits all' approach to organisational structure. The appropriateness of any given structure will depend on the organisation's culture, the environment they operate in and their industry. Fundamentally, we must remember that organisations are groups of people who are ultimately working towards a common goal, and work psychologists can add significant value by supporting organisational leaders to refocus on the human elements of what makes organisations successful or otherwise.

RECOMMENDATIONS FOR FURTHER READING

Bakker, A., Scharp, Y., Breevaart, K., and de Vries, J. (2020). Playful work design: Introduction of a new concept. *Spanish Journal of Psychology*, *23*, e19.

By, R. (2005). Organisational change management: A critical review. *Journal of Change Management*, *5*(4), 369–380.

Handke, L., Klonek, F., Parker, S., and Kauffeld, S. (2020). Interactive effects of team virtuality and work design on team functioning. *Small Group Research*, *51*(1), 3–47.

Parker, S., and Jorritsma, K. (2021). Good work design for all: Multiple pathways to making a difference. *European Journal of Work and Organizational Psychology*, *30*(3), 456–468.

6

LEADERSHIP, ENGAGEMENT
AND MOTIVATION

This chapter looks at how leadership impacts employees. After considering leadership theories in general, the issues of how leaders can be trained and what leadership means for power and influence in organisations are considered. The chapter then explores different motivation theories and how these can be used to improve workplace wellbeing. This section also considers psychological contracts and how breaching such a contract can affect motivation and performance. It also looks at organisational citizenship behaviours and counterproductive work behaviours and how they relate to motivation. Finally, engagement and the implications of working in teams and groups are explored with some practical considerations of how good teams are constituted and led.

Work psychologists working on leadership, engagement and motivation issues are usually working in a consultancy role supporting in-house staff to build policies, processes, physical and social environments which stimulate the conditions for work. This can have crossover with some of the work we have looked at in previous chapters such as designing training programmes, e.g., leadership development, or they may be designing job roles as covered in Chapter 5 on work design. Consequently, this chapter contains slightly more theory than previous ones because it is theory which is potentially used to problem solve across a range of organisational issues.

DOI: 10.4324/9781315169880-6

LEADERSHIP

Leadership is a process of influencing other people without coercion. It is distinguished from management in that managers have some form of alternate control over subordinates. Often managers and leaders are the same people. though, as, ideally, managers will have been promoted because of leadership ability and can use non-coercive forms of power. Leadership can come from any person, at any level of an organisation, using a range of different forms of power. Examples of non-coercive forms of power include power that comes from having expertise in an area (this may be through education, training or lived experience), referent power (this comes from being admired or liked), or legitimate power (for example being in an elected role). Some managers also have legitimate power because of how they have been appointed into that position, but leaders are only leaders because they have followers. Leadership theories have developed over time. Until the Second World War trait theories were popular, assuming people were born leaders. Post-war until the 1960s the focus was on behaviours and styles. Then until the 1980s research switched to look at how different situations required different forms of leadership, so called contingency approaches. Since the 1980s a range of theories have emerged, but interestingly, they have refocused on 'great people' now looking at charisma and transformational leadership, and it is worth emphasising that, whilst the main focus of research shifts over time, previous theories are still used and researched rather than replaced.

THEORIES OF LEADERSHIP

TRAIT APPROACHES

Trait approaches assume that leadership ability is something that people are born with. It is also sometimes referred to as the 'great man' approach and was a popular approach until roughly the 1940s. It is termed the great man approach as it fit with Western class systems which were still in place at this time. Obviously the 'man' element reflected societal sexism of the time and the notion that leaders would naturally be men. This approach is epitomised in figures such as Winston Churchill, a famous leader in the Allies throughout the Second World War, someone born into a particular social class, with its associated privileges. This approach is consistent with many religions and monarchy or otherwise hereditary-based governance systems. More modern looks at trait-based leadership pull out specific traits. For example, House et al. (1996) identify the traits of: drive, honesty, leadership motivation, self-confidence, business knowledge, creativity, flexibility and cognitive ability. Research has not demonstrated consistent patterns of traits however, though many named may seem intuitively beneficial. This initial tranche of research has been criticised for being romantic or having heroic ideas of leadership, and the paradigm of leadership research shifted, as society shifted post-war, so that situation was considered of paramount importance.

CONTINGENCY APPROACHES

The next focus started in the 1950s and looked at how different styles of leadership might be beneficial in different situations, so-called contingency approaches. The idea of person-oriented and production-oriented leadership became popular, spawning a range of diagnostic tools to assess style. Person-oriented leaders spend time focusing on their followers and their needs, building relationships. They will do things to protect followers and take time to communicate well with them. Production-oriented leaders focus on organising work, ensuring there are appropriate goals and systems in place and follow rules tightly. Sometimes these approaches are presented as opposites, but the dimensions are independent, and so it is possible for a leader to be both person- and production-oriented simultaneously. Contingency approaches argue that leaders need to be matched to the situation for optimal outcomes. Fiedler (1967) focused on how leaders' behaviours matched situation and divided the situation into specific elements. Fiedler argued that the following need to be considered: leader–follower relationships; clarity of task structure; and leader position power (does the leader have potential coercive power to reward or punish?). A range of literature has demonstrated that task-motivated leaders are most appropriate for situations that are extremely favourable, or extremely unfavourable, whereas relationship-oriented leaders work best in moderately favourable situations. The model is strong enough to have predictive power about who will succeed, however the 'black box problem' as Fiedler labelled it remains. This is, why does this approach work? It is also quite hard to see how these ideas can be used practically unless leaders are replaced when situations change.

House (1971) developed path goal theory which similarly looked at how different situations require different forms of leadership. However, this approach has more application as it considers the style of leadership which is most beneficial to adopt rather than the type of leader who is most effective. This model can be used to train leaders to adapt their leadership style. House argued there are four leadership styles. Directive leadership involves coordinating work and ensuring roles are clear. Supportive leadership aims to build good working environments. Participative leadership focuses on consultation and making sure all staff are listened to and involved in decisions. Achievement-oriented leadership is focused on goal setting and motivating followers to accept and achieve those goals. Using this model the leader would choose the most appropriate style to adopt considering factors such as what the task was, who the employees are, their relationship with employees, etc. For example, with an ambiguous task and employees with low independence desire then directive leadership would be effective. That approach would be ineffective where the task is not satisfying, though, and so a supportive style would fit better.

Whilst House's model allows for one leader to work in different circumstances this may still be practically difficult to switch your whole approach, particularly if leading different work groups, including those who might have crossovers of staff. Vroom and Yetton's (1973) contingency model of leadership is slightly more simple for a leader to use as it focuses on how much consultation to do with followers/employees specifically for decision-making. They propose seven questions which the leader can use to make that decision with the information then fed into a flow chart to dictate the approach to take. The questions look at aspects such as expertise of the leader, and whether the employees will commit to the decision, and the model states leaders can use one of five different styles which roughly equate to: decide themselves, consult individually, group consultation, facilitate or delegate.

NEW' LEADERSHIP

Since the 1980s there has been a shift, in popular culture, back to thinking about natural leaders with the reification of, often entrepreneurial, figures as great leaders. In some respects, this is back to the great man approach, although at least now there is a slight move to inclusivity in that it is 'great person' used as a term. Examples of such leaders are Steve Jobs and Bill Gates. The idea of born leaders has persisted throughout the history of leadership research though with figures such as Abraham Lincoln, Martin Luther King and Mother Teresa held up as great leaders. More recently researchers have tried to investigate and explore how overall style of leadership is important. Consideration of transactional and transformational leadership approaches has been key, with transformational being regarded as superior.

Transactional leadership covers most types of leadership theories covered. It is a form of leadership in which it is assumed that employees are not motivated by common goals but have to receive instructions on how to behave and be monitored to ensure they comply and that they have to be motivated by extrinsic rewards, e.g., pay. It can be highly effective in short-term tasks or in highly direct chain of command organisations such as food service or the military. There are four main types of transactional leadership. Firstly, contingent reward which is a straightforward approach. Leaders reward followers with bonuses, recognition or promotions for tasks well done. Leaders really can't be distinguished from managers in this approach, and they keep a close eye on employees, feeding back on performance. The second transactional style is active management by exception. This can be received badly by employees as the approach involves monitoring staff closely and intervening if there is a suggestion of a problem. Intervention might be a reprimand or a punishment. Passive management by exception is the third transactional style. It is like the second approach, but leaders give followers more freedom and only intervene when they have to. This freedom means that interventions, when necessary, tend to come later but are also negative in tone. Whilst these three approaches can feel harsh there is a clear correlation between performance and rewards, and they can be productive when there are clear rules, simple tasks and structure. The approach is good for staff who have a transactional psychological contract approach (see the motivation section on psychological contract). The final transactional style is not particularly beneficial at all and is termed laissez-faire leadership (from the French 'left to do'). In this approach leaders do not intervene and leave employees to work as they want with no feedback or interaction. It has been shown repeatedly to be ineffective and results in the lowest productivity as well as poorer employee wellbeing.

Transformational leaders also give employees much freedom, but the underlying beliefs and principles they have differ. Transformational leaders are effective when there is a relational psychological contract. The main difference is that there is trust and belief in transformational leadership approaches. Employees are regarded as motivated by intrinsic rewards and by the strength of relationships they hold, examples of famous transformational leaders include Nelson Mandela and Barack Obama. Transformational leadership is focused on responding to followers' needs rather than pursuing a personal goal. For many, transformational leaders appear to be representatives. There are four main elements to this style. The first is termed idealised influence, or in common language charisma. It is easy to see how this leadership style can be confused with the 'great man' approach, but the difference is about the role the leader plays as a pivot for change, rather than advancing set interests. The other elements also set transformational leaders apart as they concern relationships with followers and include intellectual stimulation, inspirational motivation and individualised consideration. Intellectual stimulation refers to an approach of stimulating creativity and innovation in followers, soliciting ideas from them. Inspirational motivation refers to the process of encouraging followers to commit to common goals or organisational vision. Individual consideration is how leaders support individual followers to achieve their personal and organisational goals which may be through a process of mentorship, coaching or direct support. Whilst it may initially seem that transformational leaders reflect particular personality types, the skills and approaches they use can be taught.

Leader–member exchange theory (often abbreviated to LMX) argues both that leaders don't treat all employees the same and that they shouldn't be expected to. It argues that relationships need to be built individually with each person. Leaders should aspire to have relationships which form mutual obligations though. This can be done by having mutual trust and respect. It is also helpful if both parties like each other. This in turn is a product of leaders acting competently and fairly. This model fits with research into discrimination and diversity in the workplace as it acknowledges that leaders are more likely to build relationships with people similar to themselves. The theory is not fully testable, but there is good support for the idea that leaders have in-groups and out-groups and that employees receive differential treatment as a result. LMX has been praised for recognising real-world situations and not idealising leadership. In contrast the notion of authentic leadership encourages valorisation and romanticisation of leaders. It has been presented as the most appropriate style for modern leadership. The main principle is that authentic leaders are 'true to themselves'. This is not just about doing what you, as a leader, believe to be right, though. Authentic leaders should be sincere and have high moral codes, which they live by whilst also being self-aware. It is clear that such a leader may be highly effective for followers who share the same positions but might be less so for those coming from other positions.

GLOBAL LEADERSHIP

Having followers who hold similar values to leaders can become more problematic in modern, globalised organisations. The theories of leadership explored here are based mostly on simple hierarchical organisations. This doesn't fit with many modern workplaces where individual employees may have multiple leaders for different projects they work on, at different levels of the hierarchy and potentially with very different values and approaches. Increasingly organisations work across different countries and cultures, not just in being multinationals but in that individual employees may work with leaders in different countries.

The Global Leadership and Organizational Behavior Effectiveness (GLOBE) project explored how leadership practices differed and were similar across one hundred and fifty countries, for over twenty years. It is a major initiative covering countries in each continent and over 95% of the world's population. There are a range of outputs from the project which are useful for any aspiring work psychologist to explore. The main findings are of similarities in approaches transnationally though. They have found that trustworthiness and having foresight are universally desired in leaders, for example, and that being irritable or dictatorial are universally disliked. It is worth noting that some major traits differ, though, and that there are major differences in whether some traits are valued or not, for example taking risks, being self-effacing and being compassionate.

DEVELOPING LEADERS

Because what is perceived as good leadership can vary, leadership training needs to take account of context. Whilst there are a range of formal management training programmes, with the MBA being the most recognised, there are also many opportunities to deliver training within organisations or to set up developmental opportunities rather than prescribed routes. One of the main issues with leadership training is that it is often given as a preparation for future leadership positions. This means that the theory learned or skills developed are not then used in practice and so are lost. It might be helpful to revisit Chapter 3 which considers issues around training.

Because of the issues of extinction of skills over time, most effective leadership training is given on the job. Most commonly, developmental assignments are given: smaller projects which allow employees to practise their skills and build confidence. These are also helpful in allowing relationships to build between leaders and followers before a promotion leads to a more permanent change. It also means that organisations can test out how effective internal candidates might be in new positions. Other common forms of development activity include coaching and mentoring as well as providing 360 degree feedback. The latter is a feedback collection and summarisation tool which allows individuals to hear from colleagues, subordinates, managers as well as, in some cases, customers, clients or other stakeholders. Whilst an effective tool it can be resource intensive for organisations to use for many employees at once as it requires feedback from, and so time of, many people.

LEADERSHIP AS A SOCIAL CONSTRUCT

Before concluding this section, it is important to address concerns that the very notion of leadership implies a particular way of working which results in more males in positions of power. The concept has been criticised as being a romanticisation of workplace practices and individuals and also as a means of preserving existing power structures and scapegoating some people. There have been active calls to move from focusing on charisma and look more at followership as well as to stop focusing on famous or high-profile leaders and look instead at genuine attempts to test theory rather than find supporting evidence.

In addition, Schein (1973) argues that there is a 'think manager, think male' approach in most organisations with women perceived as lacking leadership ability. Schein argues that many qualities valued societally, in males, but not in females, have overlaps with those seen as beneficial for leaders. This includes qualities such as competitiveness, aggression, ambition and self-confidence. Ryan and Haslam (2007) built on Schein's ideas, introducing the idea of 'think crisis, think female'. They argue that when there are specific, difficult problems in an organisation then a woman is more likely to be given a leadership role, a theory which has significant empirical support. As a consequence many of these women will fail, simply because any leader would fail, but their female socialisation will make them more likely to internalise that failure, rather than blaming the organisation.

There is some consensus in the academic literature about some aspects of leadership, though this is more about what not to do, rather than how to become the most effective leader. Research demonstrates more passive leadership is less effective (especially forms such as laissez-faire or management by exception). It is also clear that these more passive forms are linked to more transactional relationships and that it is most beneficial for organisations if employees have relational psychological contracts. This is particularly important for fast-changing organisations or complex job roles where it can be difficult to articulate all of the required tasks in a role.

It is also clear that leadership is something which involves different people at a range of different levels, not just those labelled manager or leader. It is important that we don't return to viewing leadership as something inbuilt and recognise that leadership skills can be developed in everyone. However, we should also note that it is virtually impossible to create leaders who are able to be effective in every situation.

MOTIVATION

Our lay definition of motivation maps quite well onto the way the term is used in research and consultancy. In relation to work motivation Pinder (2008) defines it as the 'set of energetic forces that originate both within as well as beyond an individual to initiate work-related behavior and to determine its form, direction, intensity, and duration'. Researchers then usually break down the term to study two different elements, distinguishing between extrinsic and intrinsic motivation.

Extrinsic motivation is any 'force' which is from outside the individual. In relation to work the most obvious extrinsic motivation is pay, which is often erroneously thought to be a major and sufficient motivator. Intrinsic motivation refers to the internal forces which compel an individual to work such as enjoyment in the work, sense of achievement or impact on sense of self-worth. There have been dozens of theories proposed over the last century. This section explores the most popular theories. It is worth noting that popularity does not always equate to robustness or having academic support though. Early research and experiments in motivation focused primarily on external motivation and the initial round of theories can be widely grouped as need theories.

NEED THEORIES OF MOTIVATION

Probably the most famous theory of motivation is Maslow's hierarchy of needs (1943). The theory has little empirical support and there is much counter-evidence to the model proposed, yet this remains probably the widest taught model. As a work psychologist it is worth remembering that both managers and employees are likely to have been taught this model at some time and may be quite attached to it. Therefore, it is important to reflect on how it can be adapted to use in practice. In essence the pyramid, usually used to represent the model, shows a range of human needs. It was originally suggested lower needs had to be met before higher needs became a driver, but Maslow later stated they weren't hierarchical. The needs represented on the bottom of the pyramid: physiological, security, social and esteem are regarded as deficiency needs. This means that as these needs are met they become less motivating. The final need, self-actualisation, is regarded as a being or growth need, meaning it is always motivating. One of the criticisms of Maslow's model is that individuals may give up achieving lower needs to achieve higher ones. Alderfer's (1972) ERG model developed Maslow's to address this issue. Alderfer argued individuals have three core needs which are existence, relatedness and growth. The initials from these create the ERG name. The three map quite closely onto Maslow's model. The main difference is that Alderfer argued that people are motivated to achieve all these needs simultaneously. The model has some academic support and can be helpful in practice to explore which needs aren't being met in the workplace and which managers should prioritise working on.

Herzberg's (1959) two-factor theory is also beneficial as a practical tool to assess what is missing in a workplace. Whilst there is only limited support for the model academically, it is a practical way to audit a workplace, and so can be used to consider what might be demotivating as well as what is potentially motivating. Herzberg argued that there are 'hygiene' factors: drivers which demotivate when absent. He identified seven, e.g. pay and supervisor relationships. He also investigated seven motivating factors such as status and recognition. The model is useful as it encourages the work psychologist to consider which hygiene factors might be achieved outside work and so are not influential, for example a low paid worker for a charity shouldn't be demotivated by pay if they simultaneously have an additional well paid job, but a volunteer on state benefits may be demotivated. Most need theories consider all workers as having similar motivations overall but McClelland's (1961) acquired needs theory thinks more about individuals' motivators. McClelland argued that everyone has some need for achievement, power and affiliation, but that which need dominates varies amongst people. Of the need theories this has the best academic support and also encourages the work psychologist to think about differing needs for differing workers. The next round of motivation research focused on processes and considered how motivation is impacted by other employees and how they are treated, as well as oneself.

PROCESS-BASED THEORIES

Adams' (1965) equity theory was the first motivation theory to focus on how people are impacted by how those around them are treated. Adams argued that people need to feel they are being treated justly by their organisation. He argued employees weigh up the outputs they receive (e.g. pay, status, punishments) relative to the inputs they give (e.g. time at work, effort) and compare this to their peers: looking for equitable treatment. However, this is not a straight comparison. Adams suggested some people are more impacted by inequity and others (termed entitleds) expect a higher ratio than their peers. The initial claim of the theory (people want equity) is useful for a work psychologist in designing performance systems. However, the addition considering individual differences in expectations means that a system that accommodates all cannot be produced, as accommodating entitleds means inherent unfairness. It is useful to think about how employees might reduce inequity though. Behavioural ways are fairly obvious: employees can either change their inputs (work less hard) or try to change outcomes (seek more pay) or change job for one perceived as more equitable. A work psychologist should also consider cognitive ways of reducing perceived inequity though, for example, an employee might distort what they perceive their own or another's inputs or outputs are. An example is giving people new job titles which appear to confer status. Equally an individual can change equity perception by changing comparator. Instead of comparing themselves to a particular coworker, they might compare themselves in a previous job or someone in another organisation.

Greenberg (1982) developed equity theory into organisational justice theory. This can be a more practical tool for work psychologists as it considers different forms of equity or justice, looking at how things are done, not just what the result is. Greenberg posits that three forms of justice are important, the first, distributive justice, is the outcome – the inputs and outputs which Adams considered. Equally important to Greenberg, though, are procedural and interpersonal justice. Procedural justice refers to the processes and policies of how the outputs were decided and distributed. Interpersonal justice is about how people were treated in those processes. For Greenberg people will not be motivated simply because they receive equitable outputs for their work, but only if they are given in a transparent, fair and humane way.

Most motivation theories focus on how employers can affect their employees' motivation. Vroom's (1964) expectancy or VIE theory also considers how motivation can be impacted by events prior to employment. VIE stands for valence, instrumentality and expectancy, which Vroom regards as the three components of motivation. He presents them using the formula $V \times I \times E = $ motivation, so that if any one one of the three is zero, motivation becomes zero. Expectancy refers to the belief that effort will lead to performance. Instrumentality means performance will lead to an outcome, and valence is whether that outcome will lead to a reward. What is critical about this theory is that it acknowledges that it is an employee's belief about these things which matters, rather than what the actual situation is. This shows motivating employees is more complicated than treating them well as an employer yourself. This issue of past effects on motivation will be picked up later in this section when we consider the psychological contract. There is strong meta-analytical support for the importance of valence, instrumentality and expectancy being important for motivation but much less so for the idea of the multiplication of these for motivation.

APPLICATION-BASED THEORIES

More recently motivational theorists have focused on the practicalities of how work psychologists and managers can support motivation. Locke and Latham (1990) proposed the importance of goal setting in this process. The concept of goal setting is well researched and well supported by the literature. In summary, the research demonstrates that it is most motivating for individuals to have difficult and specific goals. It is important that they feel attainable for the individual though, and, ideally, they should be set by the individual themselves. However, goals set by others have been shown to be equally effective if the individual agrees with them. Goal setting has often been misinterpreted and has often resulted in an annual goal-setting process as part of an employee evaluation, with goals then ignored until the next appraisal. Research in this area demonstrates that for greatest efficacy the employee needs regular feedback on the goal, and smaller, shorter-term goals would be more effective, with managers providing feedback on progress. Other personal factors have been shown to feed into this process such as self-regulation, self-efficacy and goal orientation.

Feedback has been shown to be important in goal-setting theory as it allows employees to redirect efforts if things aren't going well and serves as a reinforcer of behaviour which is working. Reinforcements and incentives are important in motivation. This section started off by pointing out that pay wasn't the only or best motivator, but it is an example of a reinforcer. Pay acts as a reinforcer in several ways: firstly, it allows the employee to meet their basic needs (food, security, etc); secondly, it provides a level of status, and finally, it is an acknowledgement of good performance and so acts as praise. When a work psychologist is designing incentive systems, they need to consider how transparent the system is and the schedule of reinforcement used. Reinforcements can be highly varied, for example, a positive comment from a peer or manager, a bonus, being given responsibility for a new task. Different people will find different things reinforcing, and some of these things (extra pay, bonuses, benefits) can be scheduled in, whereas others (positive feedback) won't work if they are contrived to be at particular points in time. When scheduled, reinforcers can use different schedules. They may be received every time (continuous), e.g., you attend a marketing event for the company and receive time off in lieu. They can be fixed ratio (e.g., every five times you undertake a behaviour), fixed interval (once a week) or variable ratio (random, or at least unknown to the recipient). Readers might want to consider this in relation to equity theory as discussed and the concept of psychological contract which will now be explored.

PSYCHOLOGICAL CONTRACT

The concept of psychological contract has strong research backing and is also well established in practice, being widely used in employee management. A psychological contract is an implicit agreement between employees and employers and covers elements of the relationship which are not explicit in a formal contract. Rousseau is the preeminent researcher in this field, and for her, what is critical is that employees believe a promise has been made and that both sides are bound to that promise. For employers this is difficult because the contract is subjective and 'mutuality is not a prerequisite' (Rousseau, 1990, p. 391): an employer may have no awareness of the employee's beliefs. Examples of contract elements are: an employee believes they will be promoted in x amount of time, if they perform well; an employee believes that if they are flexible in attending an out-of-hours event, the organisation will allow them to leave work early to attend a personal event. Employees most often mention pay and fairness issues in what they regard as important in the contract whereas managers emphasise humanity and recognition. However, there is much overlap, showing that much of the content of a psychological contract is known implicitly or explicitly by both parties. Research explores who the employee is contracting with (anthromorphised organisation, line manager, hiring manager) as well as what might be in a contract, and whether the organisation can have similar contracts with the individual. What is important for the work psychologist is to be aware that such contract exists and what the implications of a breach might be. Breaches of psychological contract, when sufficiently severe, have been demonstrated to impact productivity, engagement and turnover. In addition, they have been shown to cause employees to move from a relational contract (where both parties go beyond what is formally contracted and trust each other) to a transactional contract (where only contracted behaviours are performed and no extra effort is given).

ORGANISATIONAL CITIZENSHIP BEHAVIOURS (OCBS) AND COUNTERPRODUCTIVE WORK BEHAVIOURS (CWBS)

Psychological contract breaches can lead to workers engaging in fewer OCBs and more CWBs, impacting organisations in subtle ways. OCBs or organisational citizenship behaviours as they are named in the research are sometimes called discretionary or extra role behaviours in the workplace, and they often appear as an additional requirement on job descriptions. They encompass the additional tasks which are necessary for organisations to run but which are often hard to quantify. There are three main types, and all are dependent on motivated staff. Indeed, unions often effectively use removal of OCBs by their members, or 'working to rule', as a lever in their negotiations. Employees are completing their contracted tasks but nothing additional. The first type is personal support. This can include helping people on their work tasks, offering support or suggestions to help. The second form is organisational support, an example is saying positive things about the organisation, and the third type is conscientious initiative. This refers to employees persisting with difficult tasks or stepping up to solve a problem, beyond their work role. They have also been subdivided by Organ (1988) as actions which encompass altruism, courtesy, conscientiousness, sportsmanship and civic virtue. There is considerable evidence to demonstrate that motivated staff engage in more OCBs.

CWBs or counterproductive work behaviours are sometimes regarded as the opposite of OCBs. However, they are separate but related so that an individual can simultaneously engage in both OCBs and CWBs. CWB refers to actions which subtly harm an organisation. They have been linked to demotivation from work and disengagement from the organisation. They can be minor or major, indeed some such as theft or bullying can be grounds for immediate dismissal. However, like OCBs many are subtle and include withholding effort, absenteeism, spreading rumours, speaking badly of the organisation and sabotaging plans. It is important that work psychologists note that some forms of OCBs are both legal and reasonable responses. Employees can, and should be encouraged to, for example, whistle-blow on unethical work practices. It is a work psychologist's role to explore the reasons for CWBs, rather than trying to deal with their immediate expression.

USING MOTIVATION THEORY IN PRACTICE

Motivation theories are important to work psychologists in several areas of their work. They should be considered when designing reward or compensations strategies, when building appraisal and feedback systems and when designing jobs and promotions routes. They might plan to use a range of motivators broader than reinforcement such as job rotation, job enlargement and job enrichment which ensure ongoing motivation. These issues were also covered in Chapter 5 on work design.

Lack of motivation impacts much more than day-to-day productivity. It can have implications for organisational commitment and it can impact relationship with peers and customers. Lack of motivation can be linked to turnover which can be costly for organisations. As explored it can also lead to counterproductive work behaviours. Consequently, it is vital that organisations consider this as a major issue. Most motivation theories have been developed in a specific workplace context: Western, focusing on specific job roles, and primarily studied using male participants. Therefore, work psychologists need to stay abreast of recent research in wider contexts. It is especially important to think about the cross-cultural implications of motivation and expectations of the workplace. For example, much of East Asia retains a culture of employees remaining with one organisation for life, whereas in the West the rate of workplace change has accelerated in recent years with a significant minority of employees working for multiple organisations. The importance of expectations and perceived psychological contract and how it differs for different employees is vital to consider when designing systems, particularly for multinational organisations.

Many theories have been considered in this section, and Woods and West (2010) have effectively summarised the most effective strategies from them. They suggest employing the following five strategies. Firstly, employers should look for sources of demotivation and ensure employees are treated fairly. Secondly, it is important to provide a range of outcomes which are valued, for example, you may have a sales target for sales made but also for most friendly salesperson. Thirdly, employees should have appropriate goals and objectives to work towards. Fourthly, employees should receive helpful and timely feedback on their progress, and finally, jobs should be designed so that they are rewarding. However, both individual differences and cultural differences can affect motivation and strategies for motivating. Motivation and demotivation have multiple causes, and there is no one correct method a leader can use.

ENGAGEMENT

Engagement has been something of a buzz word in industry over the last two decades, taking over from motivation. The terms should not be conflated, though both link with performance and happiness in the workplace. Engagement is the extent to which people are attached to and fulfilled by their work. Researchers are particularly interested in how wellbeing links to engagement and usually adopt one of two main definitions. The first is behavioural. Kahn (1990) adopts this position, considering how people are engaged across three domains: emotionally, physically and cognitively. Schaufeli et al. (2002) take an alternate approach focusing on engagement as an attitudinal state. They define it as 'a positive, fulfilling, work-related state of mind that is characterised by vigour, dedication and absorption' (p. 74). When employers consider engagement, it is with more of a focus on overall performance and efficiencies than wellbeing. The UK government took this approach in commissioning the 2009 MacLeod Review which focused in particular on how engagement linked with productivity and competitiveness. This review found there were four main drivers of engagement. These were: whether leaders provided a strong and compelling narrative about the organisation and its trajectory; whether managers were themselves engaged and effective, supporting employees; whether employees' voice was heard and respected within the organisation; and whether the organisation demonstrated integrity between its values and behaviours.

Academic research broadly supports the ideas put forward by the MacLeod Review but puts focus on more subtle elements of the workplace. Bakker et al. (2014) summarise the literature which demonstrates that for engagement an environment needs to provide social support, coaching, performance feedback, task variety and tasks which have significance. Crucially, it is also essential that employees have a sense of control over their job content and how it is performed. It has also been demonstrated that personality type is a factor. Personality traits such as proactivity, optimism, conscientiousness, extraversion and emotional stability have all been shown to independently correlate with engagement. It should be noted though that, whilst one assumption of personality theory is that it is relatively stable in adulthood, it has also been demonstrated that poor working conditions such as bullying can lead to personality changes. Therefore, caution should be taken in assuming this correlation indicates certain personality types are more likely to express engagement rather than engaging work can impact expression of personality type.

ENGAGEMENT IMPACT ON WORK PERFORMANCE

Engagement has been demonstrated to be correlated with performance through a range of moderating variables which Bakker et al. (2014) summarise. These include happiness and energy levels, greater creativity, and increased active learning. Engagement has been shown to correlate with more OCBs, greater in-role performance and, subsequently, greater client satisfaction. However, it is worth noting that not all employees aim, or want, to be engaged. As discussed in the motivation section some employees hold and desire only transactional relationships with their organisation: performing the tasks they are contracted to do and keeping work and life as entirely separate domains. For some employees this transactional approach is a direct attempt to resist burnout.

Burnout is regarded by many, though not all, researchers and theorists as the opposite of engagement. When an employee experiences burnout they have no energy and feel exhausted, experiencing cynicism towards their role and seeking to create distance. It results from chronic unmanaged stress, which may originate from the workplace or elsewhere. Bakker and Demerouti (2007) outlined the job demands–resources model which considers factors impacting engagement and exhaustion. Bakker and Demerouti explain that effort in a job role comes from many areas including physical, social, psychological and organisational pressures and that different jobs will have different balances of demands. They term these job demands and argue that demands can have a negative impact if employees don't have the necessary resources to meet the demands. Resources, in this model, can incorporate many different things such as effective leadership, support of colleagues and even physical health. It is a well-supported model and is useful for work psychologists as it is highly practical. They can audit existing demands and resources in given roles and then modify roles accordingly. There are also a range of tools developed to assess both engagement and burnout that can be used as part of this audit process.

ASSESSING ENGAGEMENT

One of the first measures developed for assessing engagement was the Gallup 12. It is quick to use as it only has twelve questions, examples are: 'At work, I have the opportunity to do what I do best every day' and 'At work, my opinion seems to count'. It has been criticised as measuring job satisfaction rather than engagement, though, and focusing on the factors linked to engagement rather than engagement directly. The Utrecht Work Engagement Scale is a more direct measure of engagement asking respondents to rate statements such as 'I find the work that I do full of meaning and purpose' and 'My job inspires me'. Whilst originally containing seventeen statements it has subsequently been reduced to only nine so is again easy to use at work. Accurately measuring engagement is likely to be difficult, whatever the measure, though as there is some evidence that feelings of engagement are more related to individual traits than the specific environment. In addition, the construct of engagement has overlaps with a range of other concepts such as satisfaction, organisational commitment and job involvement. Even with these limitations it can be a useful metric to assess in organisations in order to plan improvements.

GROUPS AND TEAMS

There are some paradoxes between what people want from leaders and what good leadership practices are. We have seen through this chapter that followers value strong individual leaders whom people can respect and identify with but who are strong willed enough to push through difficult or radical changes. We have also seen through motivation research that people need collaborative work, their ideas to be valued and to have a collective sense of responsibility and own-ership of change to get behind it. For these reasons it is important that groups and teams are considered so that staff work together, thinking isn't siloed, and leadership can emerge from different levels and sections of an organisation: not just from those appointed as managers.

DIFFERENCES BETWEEN GROUPS AND TEAMS

The difference between groups and teams is about the depth of the interdependency between members. Groups are when people work towards a common goal, interacting with each other to do so. Teams similarly have common goals, but they work intensively with each other to achieve those, with mutual accountability, shared objec-tives and performance goals and a sense of shared identity. In effec-tive teams, each team member has a defined role and understands the roles of others. Teams are particularly useful in the workplace when there are complex tasks to be completed or when outcomes benefit from diverse inputs. They are also useful when work has interdepend-ent subtasks or when staff would benefit from learning opportunities from each other. The idea of a team initially implies that people work physically alongside each other. However, high-performing teams can work with team members never meeting if they have shared identity and responsibility.

Such a distinction suggests that groups and teams are binary oppo-sites. In reality there are many groups labelled as teams within organi-sations and many steps between the two structures. For example, a group working on marketing may be labelled the marketing team. It can be individuals all working on separate, independent tasks (albeit with a common aim) but with no collective responsibility. It is impor-tant that work psychologists investigate the true structure of working groups when helping an organisation to establish the genuine inter-dependence they have. A stepping stone between groups and teams is working groups. These are individuals working collectively, usu-ally on a temporary basis but often on individual independent tasks. Work psychologists can help organisations to move towards higher performing teams. Effective teams tend to be between five and twelve people. Fewer than that means that there is insufficient diversity, and greater than twelve can lead to conflict or subgroups forming. Each team should have a balance of homogeneity (which helps cohesion) and heterogeneity (which leads to greater differences in perspectives and therefore creativity potential).

IMPLICATIONS OF TEAMWORK RESEARCH ON LEADERSHIP PRACTICES

Early research on teams considered them as simply a form of group or crowd, considering them as homogeneous. Indeed, early researchers and theorists portrayed individuals as subsumed when within a group or crowd with their behaviour becoming irrational and dictated by the mass. Guidance around managing disaster situations similarly focused on the need to calm and control individuals. Research on both crowd behaviours and groups more generally over the past two decades has demonstrated clearly that individuals retain their own identity and motivations even in large crowds and that keeping them informed of the situation is most important for safe outcomes as individuals aim to help and usually stay calm. What is germane for the work psychologist is that teams are made of individuals, and leaders need to work to build effective chemistry and relationships between those individuals. Effective teams have effective communication both within and outside the team situation. Ensuring stimulation of that communication beyond the formal meetings is therefore important.

Leaders also need to ensure that all team members have psychological safety in their teams. The concept of psychological safety is relatively new but has gained significant academic support in the last ten years. Psychological safety has two components. The first is interpersonal trust. This means team members must feel confident about speaking without recriminations within their group. The second element is mutual respect. The most obvious example of this is that team members must actively listen to each other and take on board teammates' ideas. Leaders need to work to develop a sense of psychological safety across all of their followers, even when they aren't actively working in teams, in order that teams can be rapidly formed when needed to address particular issues or projects. Leaders can enhance the feeling of safety by effectively communicating themselves, addressing any issues of uncertainty or concern by followers, explaining processes and systems, and debriefing teams.

This is something which can be hard for line managers to do independently of the wider organisation and psychological safety should be an organisational level imperative.

SUMMARY

In this chapter different theories of what features an effective leader has were explored, firstly considering the idea of a born or natural leader and then exploring the features of good leadership and how those might be taught. How to increase motivation was then discussed by looking at motivation theories as they developed chronologically and built from each other. Need-based, process-based and application-based theories were all explored before looking at how psychological contracts might impact motivation and how organisational citizenship behaviours might be affected by motivation.

What engagement actually is was then discussed before looking at how it can impact work performance and how it can be assessed using short work-based tests. Finally, groups and teams were explored, starting with a discussion of how the two differ and then looking at how leaders can support teams so that they are effective, have high levels of wellbeing and are productive.

RECOMMENDATIONS FOR FURTHER READING

Hansbrough, T., and Schyns, B. (2010). *When Leadership Goes Wrong: Destructive Leadership, Mistakes, and Ethical Failures*. Charlotte, NC: Information Age.

Storey, J., Hartley, J., Denis, J.-L., and 't Hart, P. (2017). *The Routledge Companion to Leadership*. London: Routledge.

Stothart, C. (2023). *Motivation: The Ultimate Guide to Leading Your Team*. London: Routledge.

WORK PSYCHOLOGY RESEARCH AND PRACTICE

Psychologists are scientists whose role it is to understand the human experience and behaviour. For work psychologists, this investigation is generally centred on these phenomena in and related to the workplace. Therefore, as researchers and practitioners, we should follow a scientific approach, often referred to as the 'hypothetico-deductive method' when focusing on quantitative research. What this means in plain English is that psychologists should carefully define what they're measuring (which can be a challenge in itself – see Chapter 4 for wellbeing as an example), precisely measure it and then logically test hypotheses which have been developed from theories. Comparatively, when conducting qualitative research, psychologists take an inductive (rather than deductive) approach where they look in detail at a phenomenon from the bottom up. These rigorous approaches to gathering, analysing and understanding data are part of what sets psychologists apart from people who use 'common sense' explanations of human behaviour in the workplace – which can lead to false assumptions which lack evidence to back them up (Coolican, 2017). However, maintaining scientific rigour can be easier said than done in workplaces where there are literally hundreds of competing priorities, meaning that carefully obtaining data and testing it to inform decisions can sometimes be impossible. That said, it is the role of work psychologists to adhere to best practice wherever possible, and that

DOI: 10.4324/9781315169880-7

is what will be introduced in this chapter on research and practice, alongside the practical considerations of doing so.

This chapter describes the key aspects of psychological theories and looks at philosophies in conducting psychological research. We will discuss different research methods and designs used by work psychologists and the pros and cons of each, then look at how data can be collected during research. How these approaches can be applied by psychologists will be discussed, and finally this chapter will introduce how research and practice are (or should be) intrinsically linked in work psychology.

THEORIES IN WORK PSYCHOLOGY

Like many subdisciplines of psychology, work psychologists in research rarely wear white coats and protective goggles, or work in laboratories (you'll more often spot them, funnily enough, in business attire). What they *do* do, however is generate theories, gather information relating to a theory and then analyse that data to tell us something about the human condition or experience that we didn't know before – as all scientists, including work psychologists, should.

WHAT IS A THEORY?

A psychological theory can be defined as 'an organised collection of ideas that serves to describe, explain or predict what a person will do, think or feel' (Arnold et al., 2016, p. 35). A theory in work psychology should therefore be able to fill in the blanks: 'if _____, then people will _____'. Arnold and colleagues outline five elements which need to be included in theories for them to be successful, which have been adapted below:

1. The specific behaviours, thoughts or emotions which are significant to people in the workplace
2. Any differences between people in terms of how much they tend to display these behaviours, thoughts or emotions
3. Any things that happen that might influence whether these behaviours, thoughts or emotions occur
4. The consequences of the interaction between how much people characteristically display behaviours, thoughts or emotions (2) and things that happen to influence them (3)

5. Any ways in which behaviours, thoughts or emotions happening might feed back to create change in how much people characteristically display (2) them or situations that influence them (3).

As an example, imagine that a work psychologist is trying to predict how many years employees will stay in their jobs. Relevant behaviours, thoughts and emotions of individuals may include their attitude to work (e.g., a job vs a career), their level of job satisfaction, and the extent to which they are organised and punctual (1 and 2). Situations that may influence these might be the presence or absence of flexi-time, their commute to work and the colleagues that they work with (3). Any of these factors alone might impact on how many years an employee will stay in their role, but so might the interaction between these factors (4). For example, if an employee is disorganised and not always punctual but works on flexi-time where it is acceptable to come to work later and then stay late to make up the time, they may have higher job satisfaction than someone who is disorganised and late and isn't on flexi-time, so is frequently told off by their manager. This in turn may feed back to how they feel about their role, perhaps turning it from what they had once thought of as a career into 'just a job' until they can find something better (5), which would impact on that person's thoughts, behaviours and emotions towards that role (1 and 2) … and so on.

While this example is rather simple to help you get to grips with the concept, importantly good theories will be based on prior evidence and research – there should be some scientific precedent to expect the relationships that are being predicted. While this has generated some criticism (e.g., Cassell and Symon, 2004, suggested that this approach causes psychologists to be over-conservative, tweaking just a variable here or there), researchers should also consider the broader context of the area they are working in. As an example, as we move into the 2020s considerations such as remote working, older generations (aged 65+) remaining in the workplace alongside younger generations (aged ≤18) entering the workplace, and the use of technology to enable and speed up work have become so widespread that they are the norm, so theories should be shaped with these contextual factors in mind.

EVIDENCE-BASED PRACTICE: 'THAT'S ALL GOOD IN THEORY, BUT …'

Keeping at the forefront of our minds that work psychology is an applied science, we must now ask ourselves what value evidence from theories brings to practice. There is widespread agreement that work psychologists should commit to evidence-based practice, defined by Briner, Denyer and Rousseau (2009, p. 19) as being

about making decisions through the conscientious, explicit, and judicious use of four sources of information: practitioner expertise and judgement, evidence from the local context, a critical evaluation of the best available research evidence, and the perspectives of those people who might be affected by the decision.

In reality, organisations are often under pressure to improve performance while reducing costs (Kelliher and Anderson, 2010), which can impact on practitioners' ability or inclination to draw upon these information sources to make decisions. This is becoming ever more true in the ongoing unstable economic environment in the UK following the slow recovery from 2008's recession and the financial consequences of Brexit and the Covid-19 pandemic. As a result, *why* or *how* something works can be of less interest to managers and those in charge of the purse strings than the fact that it does work (and thus makes their numbers look better). Indeed, Garman (2011, p. 129) claimed that 'practitioners … rarely look to academia for practical insights', arguing that the need to deliver speedy and cost-effective solutions wins over the use of evidence-based practice. While practical in some regards, this approach of focusing on the outcome at the expense of the reasons why something may be happening runs the risk of ignoring important advances going on in work psychology research that would help to inform, and likely improve, how things are done in practice.

Take, for example, the construct validity of a psychometric test (the extent to which it is measuring what it claims to be measuring) – in this instance let's use the example of tests measuring attention to detail for use in selection. If there are two tests available to the company to use, one which costs £2.50 per employee and one which costs £12.50 per employee, which will the manager find more attractive? Of course, the cheaper option. Consider, however, if the cheaper option doesn't actually measure attention to detail properly – instead it is measuring people's perseverance because it is a long test and presents the test taker with lots of similar, tedious situations. Imagine that the work psychologist involved points out that theory and research evidence tell us that perseverance and attention to detail are two distinct constructs and do not predict the same behaviours which might impact on job performance, however the manager believes that this is simply a case of semantics and decides to go ahead with the cheaper test. Now imagine that the test is being included as part of selection for the role of a pharmacist, where attention to detail is crucial to ensure that people are being administered the correct medicines in the correct dosages. The test is successful in selecting people out of the process because it generates a range of scores that allows people who scored lower to be sifted out before getting to interview. However, in this situation, what are the potential implications of having ignored theory and evidence, and having gone for the most seemingly 'practical' approach which seemingly produces the desired outcome (narrowing down the applicant pool)? In the worst-case scenario, someone could die by being given incorrect medicine or too high/low a dosage from a pharmacist who lacks attention to detail.

Indeed, in recent years work psychologists and the associated professional bodies have become ever more concerned about the seeming lack of connection between those who discover new facts (researchers) and those who could put them into use in the workplace (practitioners) (Adams and Miller, 2008). As Arnold et al. (2016) note, the complexity of psychological theories can mean that widely applicable 'off the shelf' solutions are few and far between which means that managers and other non-psychologists may use their 'gut feel' rather than using evidence-based approaches and existing (or new) knowledge to produce solutions.

However, Bartlett and Francis-Smythe (2016) questioned whether this picture is really as bleak as it has been painted to be and examined the extent of the 'researcher–practitioner divide' and the lack of evidence-based practice in work psychologists. They found that practitioners did report consulting a range of types of evidence including reference books, research reports from sources that weren't academic journals, and empirical research papers (indeed, 71% of the sample reported using these once a month or more). The authors concluded that that the evidence used is translated into 'solutions which are both acceptable from the client perspective and consistent with the scientific standards underpinning professional knowledge and expertise in [work] psychology' (2016, p. 615) – suggesting that there is hope for research being disseminated to practitioners and being used in organisations. Nonetheless, Bartlett and Francis-Smythe did support previous researchers' concerns that client lack of interest and also the time and cost associated with accessing, searching for, finding and reading relevant evidence were barriers to using evidence in practice (Silzer et al., 2008; Cascio and Aguinis, 2008). It seems the challenge of making research accessible to all and of perceived relevance to clients remains true.

PHILOSOPHIES OF PSYCHOLOGICAL RESEARCH

As you'll have gathered from reading this book, work psychology is an incredibly broad subdiscipline of applied psychology which covers many different areas. This breadth continues into psychologists' views on how we should conduct research relating to humans in the workplace.

The English Oxford Living Dictionary defines research as: 'The systematic investigation into and study of materials and sources in order to establish facts and reach new conclusions.' Li, Easterby-Smith and Bartunek (2009) suggest that there are two polar opposite views of how this investigation should be conducted, which they describe as positivism versus social constructionism. The key differences between these two approaches are outlined in Table 7.1.

Importantly, many researchers now incorporate elements of both philosophies in their studies (and we'll look at how this can be done later in the chapter) – but if you think about the published articles you have read during your undergraduate psychology degree, it's likely that most took a positivist approach. Some researchers have started to question this stance on publication, for example Webster (2016) (who, although writing in the *British Medical Journal*, makes points that are highly relevant to work psychology and many other disciplines) noted that the sociologist Max Weber argued that research is scientific if it offers a systematic approach to researching questions and problems. Webster claimed that it is unacceptable to categorise all qualitative research as 'exploratory' and dismiss its contributions as not being 'generalisable', and argued that 'the decision to publish research should be based on standards of excellence and rigour appropriate to each approach and not be narrowly confined to positivist quantitative studies alone' (2016, p. 352).

Continuing the example of how long people stay in a role for, Table 7.2 shows some example research questions and applications from each philosophy:

TABLE 7.1 Key differences between positivism and social constructionism as philosophies of psychological research

Positivism	Social constructionism
Reality is objective	Reality is subjective (socially constructed)
Usually measured quantitatively (using numbers)	Usually measured qualitatively (using words)
Rules out alternative explanations of findings	Meaning of events and constructs are interpreted by people
Aims to measure facts	Aims to understand experiences
Researcher as separate from the investigation	Researcher as an influencer of the findings

TABLE 7.2 Examples of positivism and social constructionism in practice

Philosophy	Research question	Application of findings
Positivism	Is the relationship between employees' organisational skills and their tenure moderated by flexi-time?	Implementing flexi-time to improve tenure Selecting more organised employees
Social constructionism	What is the experience of employees in relation to their perceived organisational skills and flexi-time at work?	Wellbeing interventions for employees finding organisational aspects of work stressful

While some have criticised the over-reliance on positivism in psychological research and practice – arguably generating a certain 'type' of person who become work psychologists, what we are trying to show you here is that both have their place in work psychology (both in practice and published research), and by using the approaches together we can begin to build a more full understanding of particular phenomena and human experiences in the workplace.

PLANNING RESEARCH IN WORK PSYCHOLOGY

When planning research, every aspect of research design should be guided by the research question. Importantly, although preparing for

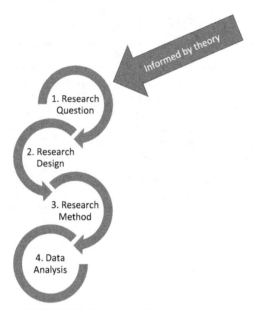

FIGURE 7.1 The hierarchy of research

data analysis should come last in terms of the order in which research is planned, it's crucial to ensure *before* data collection starts that the researcher is gathering everything they need to be able to analyse the data in a way that answers their research question(s). It's very challenging (and sometimes impossible) to go back to participants and collect further data once they have already taken part in research (for example people may change jobs, be unavailable or simply unwilling to give more time), so it's vital to ensure that work psychologists have thought through all four stages of their research before beginning.

DEVELOPING A RESEARCH QUESTION

The flow chart below gives a simple example of how you might go about developing a research question (or questions) in your own work. Research questions are the questions you are trying to answer about human beings in the workplace by gathering and analysing the data you have.

1. Choose a topic of interest: The topic that you're exploring should be of interest to you. Think who else would be interested in the

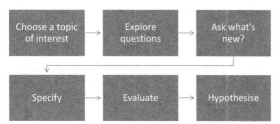

FIGURE 7.2 A process for developing research questions

outcomes of research on this topic? What is known so far on the topic? What remains unclear or unknown? As you'll see in Figure 7.3, this may be driven by what's happening in your workplace, or researchers may be approached by a company who want to know more about something they're observing in their own workplace. Alternatively the topic may be entirely theory-driven, based on furthering existing research primarily out of academic interest.

2. Explore questions: Ask 'how' and 'why' open-ended questions about this topic, drawing on existing research about the area of enquiry. Use resources such as online databases, books and your own network.

3. What's new? Ask if we already know the answer to the questions you're asking – what is the question adding to existing knowledge? For example is there a new sample or new industry being explored? Do we know the cause and effect of a phenomenon but not employees' experience of it?

4. Specify: Narrow down and determine your exact research question(s).

5. Evaluate: Check the quality of your research question(s):
   - Is the question clear (i.e. is it easily to understand what it is asking?)
   - Is the question focused (i.e. is it specific enough to research and answer?)
   - Is the question sufficiently complex (i.e. a yes/no answer is too simple to build research around)
   - Can the question be measured by obtaining and analysing data (i.e. is it answerable with the resources available to you as a researcher?)

6. Hypothesise: This is about anticipating what the data will tell you in answer to your research question – making a prediction about your findings.

(adapted from George Mason University Writing Center, 2008)

CHOOSING A RESEARCH TOPIC: THE DIVIDE

Many work psychologists and the organisations they work with have commented on the seeming 'disconnect' between researchers and practitioners in this field when it comes to choosing a topic of research, gathering data and applying it.

Hodgkinson and Herriot (2002) distinguish between two ways of doing research in work psychology, as shown in Figure 7.3.

Both of these approaches have their advantages and disadvantages. While scientific enquiry generally has more carefully defined variables and units of measurement, based on prior research, it can be disconnected from the people who are intended to be the 'end users' of the outcomes of the research – i.e., practitioners who can implement the findings into the workplace. Arguably then, scientific enquiry can produce robust evidence which furthers theory and research – but perhaps for problems and solutions that are less pressing to those in the workplace, as it is often not planned in collaboration with stakeholders. The way in which scientific research is disseminated can also present a challenge – typically managers (and very often work psychologists too!) don't have access to academic journals as they require paid subscriptions and so do not benefit from the knowledge being shared in this way. However, there is a growth in free access journal articles and online databases such as Google Scholar which are increasingly making knowledge more accessible to those who know where to search for it. In the UK, the higher education Research Excellence Framework (REF) is an expert review of the quality of outputs from higher education institutions, including academic publications and their impact beyond academia. In order for outputs to be eligible for counting towards an institution's REF score, they are required to be

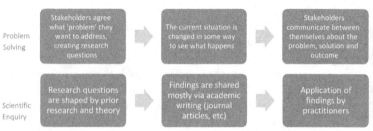

FIGURE 7.3 Two approaches to doing research in work psychology

Open Access (meaning that with internet connection can search for them and for them to be discoverable via search engines). In theory this means that the academic literature and latest research are available to a much wider audience; however, a degree of existing knowledge is still required to 1) know where to look for such evidence, and 2) know how to interpret and apply it.

On the other hand, the problem-solving approach does typically involve stakeholders and so may address more 'real-life' issues. However, due to the reasons discussed earlier in this chapter, the research design may be less likely to follow best practice (such as ensuring that the measures used have construct validity, that participant numbers are sufficient for psychometric analysis, that possible confounding variables are controlled for, and so on). So there is arguably some trade-off between scientific rigour and applicability of research findings when looking at these two approaches. Of course these limitations can be overcome by greater involvement of stakeholders in research design, encouraging organisations to take a long-term view of the challenges they are facing and to spend more money where needed to ensure that findings are valid – however, in reality these can be challenging to achieve with so many competing priorities to consider on both sides. Indeed, writing about applied psychology more broadly, Cascio and Aguinis (2008) identified a fall in practitioners being involved in published research since the 1960s, and today we are arguably in no better a position (Cortina et al. 2017). Work psychologists should ensure that they are balancing between scientific rigour and pragmatism as far as possible, rather than favouring one over the other for convenience or ease. We should also seek to blend research and practice rather than seeing them as distinct areas or professions: practitioners have much to add to researchers' knowledge and understanding of work psychology and vice versa.

RESEARCH METHODS IN WORK PSYCHOLOGY

Now that we understand the philosophies behind research in work psychology, and the approaches to doing research in practice, let's look at how psychologists go about conducting research – the *methods* they use. In other words, the ways in which information is gathered before it is analysed. Note that this is different from research design, which is linked to how data will be analysed – we'll come on to this later.

QUESTIONNAIRES

Questionnaires typically take the form of written questions (either paper and pencil or online) and are often used in work psychology research. Constructs measured by questionnaires include (but are not limited to) attitudes, beliefs, opinions and experiences. *Structured questionnaires* allow the respondent to choose between multiple options predefined by the researcher (e.g., 1–5, true or false) – also known as 'closed questions'. *Unstructured questionnaires* have open-ended questions which allow respondents to write answers in their own words.

Pros

Questionnaires of this nature are typically unsupervised, meaning that respondents can complete them as and when they want. This convenience can allow researchers to access larger sample sizes as it doesn't require them to be physically present to collect the data – respondents can simply submit it online or send the hard copy back to the researcher.

Cons

The lack of supervision can mean that respondents may not take the questionnaire as seriously and consequently may provide less valid data if they are distracted – they may even get someone else to do it for them, although that is less likely for questionnaires than psychometric tests (below). This also removes control from the researcher regarding how many people provide data and when, as it is up to the respondent to decide whether and when to send their data to the researcher.

PSYCHOMETRIC TESTS

When they were first developed, psychometric tests were similar to structured questionnaires taken under supervised conditions. These tests measure aptitude, ability and personality and are often used in recruitment settings or for development. For this reason, it is important to get as close as possible to a true measure of someone's score on these constructs, and so they are sometimes (but not always) administered in invigilated circumstances. More recently, game-based psychometric tests have become popular in the marketplace, though they still represent a small part of the overall psychometric market. These game-based measures track patterns in how people respond as they move through a game or activity, for example picking up if they are particularly hesitant, risk-tolerant, innovative or good at problem solving. In this way their actual behaviours are measured, rather than their perceptions of their behaviour as with traditional personality psychometrics. More detail on the use of psychometrics for selection purposes is available in Chapter 2.

Pros

Unlike some other measures, psychometric measures provide primary evidence (i.e., of actual behaviours) of aptitude, personality and ability. As psychometrics are increasingly being completed in uncontrolled conditions, people can take them at their own convenience (this is especially the case for game-based assessments that can be completed on a mobile device).

Game-based psychometrics allow organisations to gather huge amounts of data about an individual from a relatively short test, are engaging and harder to cheat on than other measures.

Cons

Traditional paper-and-pencil-based psychometric tests can be lengthy and tedious to complete, which may translate to fewer participants completing the tests, and therefore fewer data as an output of the research. There are also arguments that psychometric tests of aptitude and ability adversely impact (i.e. unfairly disadvantage) certain ethnicities (e.g., Jencks and Phillips, 2011), therefore skewing the data in a way that does not accurately represent the sample's true scores.

INTERVIEWS AND FOCUS GROUPS

Arguably a key skill for work psychologists is to be able to conduct interviews on a one-to-one basis, or in group settings (also known as focus groups). Similar to questionnaires, interviews can be structured or unstructured depending on the type of data that needs to be collected and the research question. Semi-structured interviews are in between these approaches, whereby the interviewer asks a set question and then uses different probes depending on how the respondent answers. Interviews typically obtain large amounts of verbal data, which can be recorded by researchers taking written notes or using audio recording devices.

Pros

Interviews can provide rich information that is difficult to obtain in other ways. They also have the benefit that interviewees can talk freely in their own words thus giving their own view, which other methods are less able to achieve.

Cons

Compared to other forms of data collection, interviews are time-consuming and labour-intensive as they require the interviewer to conduct the interview and then write up notes (known as the interview transcript if taken verbatim from a recording). This can be less attractive to researchers wishing to obtain lots of data quickly.

DIARIES

One approach to collecting rich data 'from the horse's mouth', without having to arrange a time for both the researcher and the person taking part in the research to be available, is to use diaries. These can be once a day, multiple times a day or less frequent, and are often used when researchers want to capture data about certain phenomena over time.

Pros

Using diaries doesn't require the researcher to physically be with the participant to obtain data, which means that it can be possible to collect rich, individualised data from multiple participants at any one time (in a way that is not possible with interviews, for example). It's possible to track changes in participants' thoughts, feelings and so on over time if they send their diary entries back to the researcher as soon as they've written them.

Cons

With the benefit of the researcher not needing to be present comes the drawbacks of diaries – participants can forget (or simply not be bothered!) to complete their diary entries. As the researcher isn't present to keep the participant on topic, the data collected may not directly relate to the area of study. Compared to interviews and multiple-choice questionnaires, diaries also arguably require more effort from participants as they have to write things down in detail. Finally, diaries can also be subject to 'goldbricking' whereby people may over-inflate the realities of their work role by fictionalising elements to make it sound more interesting, busy or dynamic than it really is.

PSYCHOPHYSIOLOGICAL AND PSYCHOPHYSICAL MEASURES

These measures assess the properties of the body at a biochemical and anatomical level in response to external events, typically in laboratory environments. They observe activity in muscles and sweat glands, eye movements, cardiac response, blood pressure, electrical activity in the brain, respiration and more.

Pros

This type of method produces 'hard data' which is arguably more robust than non-laboratory-based data collection.

Cons

These measures are less commonly used in work psychology because they require special equipment that is difficult to move into workplaces and is expensive. Obtaining the data can be stressful for those being measured, and the resulting data is often perceived to be less immediately applicable to work contexts than it is to other areas of psychology (e.g. cognitive or social psychology).

OBSERVATIONS

In the context of work psychology, this often takes the form of observing people completing their jobs (either to analyse the tasks involved in the role, known as *job analysis*, or to take a measure of someone's performance in the job). In these situations, the people being observed are usually informed in advance and have consented to having data collected about them.

Pros

Observation allows researchers to collect information about what is said and done first hand, in a way that is practically impossible with all other methods. Rich and detailed information can be obtained without the person being observed having to stop what they're doing (which can also be looked upon favourably by managers who want their employees to be productive!).

Cons

Without clear goals and objectives for the purpose of the observation, the amount of data collected can be enormous and difficult to manage. The person being observed is likely to act differently (perhaps on their 'best behaviour') when being observed which can mean that the data obtained is less accurate. Again, this is a time-consuming method of collecting information as it requires the researcher to be physically present, and they can typically only observe one or two people at any one time.

WHICH PHILOSOPHY, WHICH RESEARCH METHOD?

Thinking back to earlier in this chapter where we discussed positivism and social constructionism in work psychology, you may have already started to think about which methods are best suited to which philosophical standpoint. As Table 7.3 shows, most methods can be appropriate for both approaches to research, depending on how they are designed and applied.

Taking questionnaires as an example, structured questionnaires tend to acquire numerical data, meaning that they don't give rich data about *why* things occur (social constructionism) – simply whether or not they do (positivism). As another example, an interview for a job analysis which aims to understand the tasks involved in a role and the responsibilities someone has takes a positivist standpoint (the researcher wants to know the *facts* about what happens in that role and

TABLE 7.3 Research methods and philosophical approaches

Research method	Positivist	Social constructionist
Questionnaires		
structured	✓	
unstructured		✓
Psychometric tests	✓	
Psychophysiological and psychophysical measures	✓	
Observations	✓	✓
Interviews		
structured	✓	✓
unstructured		✓
Focus groups	✓	✓
Diaries	✓	✓

is not necessarily interested in the interviewee's personal reflections on *why* that is the case). On the other hand, an interview that is seeking to understand the experience of individuals working in a specific role will be less interested in the facts about the job itself, and more concerned with how the interviewee personally experiences them.

WHAT SHOULD I TAKE INTO CONSIDERATION WHEN CHOOSING A RESEARCH METHOD?

There are lots of factors that will impact which research method(s) you use, but a few have been listed below to start you thinking:

- The time you have for data collection
- Which methods your participants are most likely to engage with (if in practice)
- Which obtains the type of data you need to answer your research question(s)
- The way you want to analyse your data
- The time available for data analysis.

RESEARCH DESIGN

Now that we've outlined some different types of research methods, let's discuss what we mean by research *design*. In brief, design is the level above the methods you use, and relates to the overall plan about how you are going to answer your research question. Although closely related, research design is a *plan* to answer your research, and the methods are how you are actually going to *implement* that plan. Some research designs are presented below – note this isn't an exhaustive list but should help to get you thinking about how to frame your research.

SURVEY DESIGNS

As Arnold et al. (2016) note, one of the key features of survey designs is that they do not intervene or control naturally occurring events; instead they simply take a measure of what's naturally occurring at a given time by asking people to report on it. Most commonly this collects quantitative data using questionnaires which allows the examination of relationships between variables. However, interviews can also be used such as in market or social research.

Great for ...

- Quickly obtaining large quantities of data in organisations as surveys typically require small time investments from participants.
- Using pre-validated measures for constructs, as many such questionnaires exist.
- Gathering an initial understanding of relationships between variables, to inform further in-depth research.

Less Useful for ...

- Gathering peripheral data around research questions (as participants can only respond to the closed questions that they are asked).
- Understanding how and why relationships between variables occur (social constructionist research).

EXPERIMENTAL DESIGNS

In comparison to survey designs, the purpose of an experimental design is to control a situation and manipulate certain conditions to understand the causes of certain phenomena. While this is advantageous as it allows psychologists to gain 'purer' measures of human behaviours, this is not without its own challenges. Arguably the most pressing of these is that experimental research typically takes place in a laboratory, which is removed from the workplace environment that work psychologists should seek to apply their findings in. If employees were to be observed under experimental conditions, they would need to be in a laboratory rather than their own working environment. The first challenge this presents is cost; any time away from the workplace is a loss in productivity at the expense of the business. Another important drawback here is that that laboratories are significantly different environments compared to most working spaces – even if 'mocked up' to look more like where they typically work, this is likely to result in participants behaving or feeling differently to how they would in their typical working environment, which reduces the validity of any data collected. Alternatively, the psychologist may use participants who are not employees but are simply there to take part in the experiment which arguably reduces generalisability even further.

The psychologist will implement an intervention for the experimental group (for example, increased or decreased working hours, changes in lighting, changes in team sizes and so on) and will also have a control group of individuals (ideally matched by other relevant variables such as age and years' work experience) who will not experience the experimental intervention. The conditions experienced by the control and experimental groups should be identical apart from the intervention, which is different.

For example, imagine that a work psychologist wants to test whether increasing the number of breaks someone has in a day at work (IV) impacts on their productivity (DV) and job satisfaction (DV). Prior research has shown that age (CV) impacts on productivity (e.g., Skirbekk, 2004) and gender (CV) impacts on job satisfaction (e.g., Cottingham, Erickson and Diefendorff, 2015). Therefore,

TABLE 7.4 Types of variables in experimental design

Variable type	Description
Independent variable (IV)	The things manipulated to see if there is a resulting effect
Dependent variable (DV)	The things that are expected to change as a result of the manipulations
Control variable (CV)	The things that may impact on the relationship between the IV and DV that are not relevant to the study

the researcher would aim to match the control group (who get one 10-minute break mid-morning and a 30-minute lunch break) and the experimental group (who get one 10-minute break mid-morning, a 30-minute lunch break, and a 10-minute break mid-afternoon) as closely as possible in terms of age and gender.

In reality, *field experiments* are more often used in work psychology, where instead of using a laboratory, the experiment is set in people's actual work environments and uses naturally occurring situations as their variables. Such experiments tend to have less 'perfect' designs – for example the experimental and control groups are usually determined by the real-life situations at work and are unlikely to be matched in any meaningful way on control variables (i.e., variables that may impact the outcome of the study).

Great for ...

- Initial research in controlled settings, before applying findings in practice.
- Answering the question 'what causes x, y, z to occur?'

Less Useful for ...

- Realism/generalisation to the real world.
- Keeping costs down (unless a field experiment).
- Research questions which present ethical problems to manipulate.

CASE STUDY DESIGNS

Case studies provide an in-depth study of a particular (usually narrow) research area. They are often used to narrow down a very broad field of research into one or a handful of examples. For example, Göbel (2000) published a case study about the single owner of a car varnishing firm, 'Klaus B.', to understand his success as an entrepreneur. The author looked at Klaus B.'s motives, personality and strategies and compared these to other entrepreneurs to understand his success. Rather than answering the research question 'what makes entrepreneurs successful?' by running a large-scale study, Göbel instead used a case study design to understand one specific example of this phenomenon in detail. For this reason, case studies can be useful for testing whether a specific theory applies to phenomena in the 'real world' and is also appropriate to start to understand a subject area when little is known about it.

Great for ...

- Gaining greater understanding of a complex issue from detailed analysis of specific events and relationships.
- Using a variety of methods in combination to understand phenomena in depth.
- Learning about a relatively unknown phenomenon as a starting point for wider research ...
- ... and also gaining more in-depth understanding of something we already know about at a high level.
- Examining contemporary, 'real-life' situations to apply theory in practice.

Less Useful for ...

- Generalising findings – case studies tell us a lot about a little (rather than a little about a lot) and so cannot usually be used as evidence for validity or reliability on a wider scale.
- Strictly positivist research – the intense exposure to the topic of study that researchers have during case studies is likely to skew their interpretation of the situations and findings.
- Establishing cause and effect relationships.

ACTION RESEARCH DESIGNS

Action research means that the researcher takes part as well as the participants. In work psychology it typically takes place in the workplace and follows a cycle: both the researcher and the participants (most often employees) agree on an issue that needs to be addressed, and an intervention is planned. The intervention is then implemented (the 'action') and observations are made about its effects. Depending on the outcome, a new intervention will then be implemented and so on. Like qualitative research, it aims to understand how people taking part in the research experience things and tends to be longitudinal.

Great for ...

- Focusing on a specific problem in an organisation and identifying how to solve it.
- Unlike some other research designs, action research is collaborative and adaptive, making it more 'accessible' to communities.
- Such research often has direct and immediate impacts in practice (as we know from earlier in this chapter, this is not often the case).

Less Useful for ...

- Taking an objective view of the situation and implementation – most often the researcher is working for the organisation where the action research is happening, and so they may be under pressure to achieve certain targets or implement specific interventions (see the earlier discussion about theory informing research, though!).
- The cyclical nature of the research can mean that it is never truly finished and can therefore be very challenging to write up.

Most of the research designs discussed so far tend to lend themselves to either positivism or social constructionism – but it is possible to bridge both philosophies in research design by using multiple methodologies. In effect this is the best of both worlds because using methods from both philosophies in one's research design allows the researcher to off-set some of the limitations of each. Table 7.5 outlines some of the key strengths and weaknesses of this approach.

WHICH PHILOSOPHY, WHICH RESEARCH DESIGN?

At this point in the chapter, you will likely be able to identify which research design aligns most closely with positivism and social constructionism, but in case you need a hint, see Table 7.6.

LONGITUDINAL AND CROSS-SECTIONAL STUDIES

Finally, let's look at the differences between longitudinal and cross-sectional studies. General consensus among work psychologists is that longitudinal studies – those that take measures of the same phenomena across multiple timepoints (be that days, weeks, years or even decades) – are the best quality research. This is in comparison to

TABLE 7.5 Strengths and weaknesses of a mixed methods research design

Strengths of mixed methods designs	Weaknesses of mixed methods designs
Words, pictures and narrative can be used to add meaning to numbers	Can be difficult for a single researcher to carry out both qualitative and quantitative research; it may require a research team
Can answer a broader and more complete range of research questions because the researcher is not confined to a single method or approach	Researcher has to learn about multiple methods and approaches and understand how to mix them appropriately
A researcher can use the strengths of an additional method to overcome the weaknesses in another method	More expensive and time-consuming
Can provide stronger evidence for a conclusion through convergence and corroboration of findings	Methodological 'purists' insist that one should always work within either a qualitative or a quantitative paradigm

Johnson and Onwuegbuzie, 2004)

TABLE 7.6 Research designs and philosophical approaches

Research design	Positivist	Social constructionist
Survey	✓	
Experimental	✓	
Action research		✓
Case studies		✓
Mixed methods	✓	✓

cross-sectional research, which takes a snapshot of how things are at a single given timepoint, from one or multiple samples. Examples of longitudinal research may include examining changes in reported wellbeing of a sample over time while mapping life and work-related stressors at these timepoints also, whereas a cross-sectional equivalent would simply capture reported wellbeing and stressors at a given time and examine the relationship between these two static variables.

Longitudinal studies benefit from telling researchers about the cause and effect of relationships between variables (a sequence of events), which cross-sectional studies cannot as they are simply a snapshot in time. However, cross-sectional research designs have merit. For example, they allow researchers to look at many different variables at once with relatively little additional resource or effort (particularly if using a survey design). They are also completed more quickly than longitudinal studies and so can be used to establish whether there appear to be associations between variables, before then going on to conduct a piece of longitudinal research to establish if the relationship is likely to be causative.

Importantly, it's possible that both cross-sectional and longitudinal pieces of research are still based on theory-driven research questions and hypotheses and use appropriate methodology and analyses for the data they collect, otherwise the research will not be valuable, regardless of whether it is cross-sectional or longitudinal. No matter how sophisticated statistical techniques available today may be, none can substitute for sound design of research studies.

SUMMARY

This chapter has introduced you to the fundamentals of research and practice in work psychology: looking at the role and importance of theories to build sound research from, considering approaches to conducting research in practice, and discussing different philosophies of doing so. We've also outlined the many different types of research methods and designs used by work psychologists, along with the benefits and drawbacks of each. Throughout the chapter we've considered the challenges of conducting research as a practising work psychologist, and how we can begin to tackle these by keeping evidence-based practice at the forefront of our minds.

RECOMMENDATIONS FOR FURTHER READING

Anderson, N. (2007). The practitioner–researcher divide revisited: Strategic-level bridges and the roles of IWO psychologists. *Journal of Occupational and Organizational Psychology, 80*(2), 175–183.

Bartunek, J., and Rynes, S. (2014). Academics and practitioners are alike and unlike: The paradoxes of academic–practitioner relationships. *Journal of Management, 40*(5), 1181–1201.

Hayes, N. (2021). *Doing Psychological Research*, 2nd edn. London: McGraw-Hill Education.

THE FUTURE OF WORK PSYCHOLOGY

This final chapter draws together some of the themes from this book and explores how the current climate impacts the workplace as well as looking at what future events and movements might be important for work psychologists. It considers the impact of being in a VUCA environment (volatile, uncertain, complex and ambiguous) before exploring the impact of changing population demographics, globalisation and job polarisation. It then turns to look more specifically at the impact of Covid and ongoing effects of shifting cultural expectations around work which underpin movements such as the four-day week. The chapter, and consequently book, then closes by looking forward to how the role of work psychologist might change, and suggestions are made as to specific journals which can be used for work psychologists to keep themselves up to date on issues as they move forward in their career.

SUMMARY: THEMES EXPLORED

This book has covered a number of different discrete topics, which will be summarised here, before an exploration of the themes which underpin these. The book began with a brief exploration of what work psychology was, how one became accredited and who the key bodies for psychologists are. Chapter 2 then covered how psychological

DOI: 10.4324/9781315169880-8

assessment at work occurred more widely than initial selection and assessment work. It discussed the practicalities of selection tools but also introduced the idea of underpinning criteria which a work psychologist should use when evaluating how useful a tool was. This chapter explored the importance of considering validity and reliability as essential metrics, whilst also considering legality, fairness and criteria linked to financial efficiency such as generality of measures, practicality and costs. This brings out one of the first themes of the book: that work psychologists have to balance best practice and costs. Work psychologists are employed by organisations and have obvious financial constraints on what they can do. They must never let those constraints lead them to cut corners so that systems they design or deliver are no longer fair, valid or reliable, or so that employees are harmed.

Chapter 3 then looked at learning, training and development. It discussed the stages of this process and the factors which impacted good learning transfer. A key theme to emerge in this chapter concerned the importance of evaluation. Work psychologists should seek to evaluate all the work that they do for two key reasons. Firstly, evaluation ensures that time and resources are efficiently used. Secondly, and more importantly, evaluation ensures that there are no adverse impacts resulting from an intervention and that people from different groups are being treated equitably. Evaluation was talked about here specifically in relation to checking learning interventions but it is something that is necessary for all interventions by work psychologists.

Chapters 4 and 5 then explored wellbeing and work design respectively. Chapter 4 looked at the importance of wellbeing for work and wider life. It explored how it could be assessed, and the chapter focused particularly on stress and its effects and how it might be reduced. Chapter 5 picked up some of the same issues looking at models for designing work and how to prepare for and manage change. A major theme emerging here was about the importance of treating employees holistically, not just as 'human resources'. Work psychologists are rarely hired by employees or employee rights groups. Despite this, they should always act ethically and keep uppermost in their practice that employees are stakeholders in organisations too. The need for profit or the drivers of other stakeholders must never trump the needs of employees.

Chapter 6 then explored leadership, engagement and motivation. It introduced many theories on these topics and considered how different contexts meant that different approaches were needed. Another theme was exemplified here. Work psychologists need to ensure that they are sensitive to both contexts and individual differences. It is vital that they always closely consider the situations they are working in and how that might impact how theory is applied, and whether an intervention from another context can be transferred. This might mean exploring religious, social, economic or cultural contexts. These might all affect how employees approach work relationships and may also impact their own wellbeing in the workplace. Individual differences in employees should also be considered. Some of these seem quite obvious as they make up what is termed protected characteristics (aspects of identity which are legally protected). Examples of protected characteristics in most countries (though not all) include age, gender and sexuality. Other individual differences are less immediately apparent, these include social class, personality differences and living circumstances. It is vital that work psychologists never attempt to apply an intervention wholesale simply because it has worked elsewhere, with another group. These factors should always be considered.

Finally, Chapter 7 looked at how theories are developed and research is undertaken in work psychology. This chapter explored psychology as a science and looked at different research methods. An underpinning theme exemplified in this chapter was the need for work psychologists to use evidence-based practice. Superficially this seems obvious: psychologists should refer to the scientific evidence and consensus. The idea has been critiqued though as sometimes being at odds with the need for psychology practice to take into account contexts and individual circumstances. Professor Rob Briner is a particular advocate for evidence-based practice, and he argues that decisions should always consciously and deliberately draw out all the relevant evidence. He widens the evidence base which should be considered, arguing that practitioners, stakeholders and the organisation are also sources of relevant evidence, not just the scientific literature. He argues that practice should reflect a consideration of all the available evidence. This is particularly important when contexts and climates are rapidly changing.

CURRENT CLIMATE

Over the last twenty years there have been a range of changes in workplaces and society which mean that the current working climate can be different from that described or predicted by early theories. It is important when looking at research to always consider the context you are using that in, be that country, culture or time. This section outlines some of the changes which have occurred and how they are impacting current work practices in a VUCA world. VUCA stands for volatile, uncertain, complex and ambiguous and is an acronym coined by the military which has moved over to describe the current business environment. Volatility is about the extent to which there is unexpected and dynamic change in the workplace. This may mean work psychologists have to prepare employees for changes, redesign systems and ensure organisations are psychologically ready to make rapid changes. Uncertainty refers to the extent to which there are novel situations whose significance is not immediately transparent. For work psychologists this might mean selecting for and training people to be leaders through uncertain times. The third element of VUCA is complexity. This refers to how interconnected organisations have become with multiple intersecting elements. This might be across organisations (for example, in that they outsource functions to the same providers, or work competitively on some projects and cooperatively on others). The intersection is also about internal systems and may present itself as, for example, complex chains of command or reporting with individuals who have multiple line managers or leaders. This presents difficulties for work psychologists in designing systems and processes as the more complex systems are the more likely it is that there are unintended consequences from any change. The final element of the acronym refers to ambiguity within the organisation or wider environment. Systems that are volatile, uncertain or complex are still manageable because organisations are aware of the issues they face, even if there aren't clear paths to solve them. The added element of ambiguity is that the wider environment has unknown unknowns: things which cannot be predicted or anticipated. In ambiguous situations work psychologists may not be able to see what events are on the horizon and so are unable to plan for them. This makes issues such as workforce planning, training and engagement issues especially difficult. Ambiguity can come from factors such as: rapidly altering technology impacting businesses; changing cultural norms; war or civil unrest and climate events, to name a few. The main issue is that work psychologists may not know even what type of ambiguous events may impact. This means that on a personal level they need to be tolerant of change and uncertainty and highly resilient as they approach the issues which we are aware of. Some of these will now be considered.

POPULATION CHANGES

The global population has shifted in significant ways over the last few decades. Whilst there has been significant population growth, up to 8 billion, the rate of growth has reduced, peaking at about 2% in the 1960s. It is currently about 1.14%, and the rate is expected to continue dropping. Population growth rates are inversely correlated with female education rates, welfare safety provision in a country and country gross domestic product. Essentially as populations become richer, and healthier, they have fewer children. So, whilst ensuring all people have resources is a current issue, a longer-term one is that populations are expected to contract: a pattern already seen in highly affluent nations such as Singapore which has a −4.2% population change annually. The UK's is currently 0.4% whilst the USA's is 0.1%. Contracting populations in many Western countries, caused by birth rate decline and improved healthcare, means that there are increasing proportions of older people. Many of these will remain in the workforce, driven by the need to continue earning money, or by the desire to get the implicit benefits of work: interest and social status. Work psychologists will need to consider their needs and how existing models of motivation and learning fit. It is also important to consider what this means for promotion and the recruitment of younger people. A significant youth unemployment problem exists across Europe, exacerbated by older people not leaving the workforce and freeing up the most desirable jobs. Simultaneously lower-paid work is increasing in the form of care and service work, in part to meet the needs of an ageing population.

There are other demographic shifts in the labour force. Increasingly women are taking on traditionally male roles. Most women are in some form of work, and there is increased participation in the workforce by others who have experience discrimination in the past such as some ethnic groups and disabled people. Few models of career or theories of motivation account for people who are not traditional able-bodied male workers. Indeed, many assume that employees will have a partner who stays at home conducting practical tasks such as child-care, shopping and household management. The move to dual worker couples means that organisations need to consider practicalities which can impact them, offering flexible working hours, and services such as elder care, creches or childcare. Shifts in employees' demographics need to be actively addressed in other areas too. Diversity and equal opportunities need to be running themes through workforce planning and training. Work psychologists may also need to consider intergroup relations in the workplace.

GLOBALISATION AND INTERNATIONALISATION

The advent of globalisation and internationalisation of organisations themselves and of customer and client bases has had several impacts. These include financial pressures, increasing workloads for individuals, changed workforces and delayered organisations. Organisational drives to cut costs to be able compete, financially, in a global marketplace can lead to changes in how jobs are performed and can push innovation and creativity. They may also lead to mechanisation of process or the use of technology to support work more generally. This brings training needs as well as the need for effective and accurate job design to make sure that workers can interface with technology well. Financial pressures can also lead to increased pressures on individuals. Work psychologists may need to work with organisations to ensure that mental wellbeing isn't impacted, and that stress is not just tolerable but is at optimal levels for work. There is a risk of overloading employees leading to burnout, psychological contract breaches as a result and therefore poorer working relationships. This in turn impacts wellbeing and productivity. Internationalisation also means that organisations might have cross-cultural teams working and individual employees might work transnationally, either relocating or working virtually. This brings many issues with which work psychologists can help such as ensuring local context of policies and processes are considered, for example in selection or training. They may also help in ensuring there is effective communication and teambuilding across the organisation. Finally, a major product of internationalisation is that organisations have changed in structure. Increasingly they are flatter, with fewer levels and some functions outsourced. This has implications for the work psychologist's own role. They are more likely to be external consultants rather than in-house employees. Human resource service is one of the functions most likely to be outsourced, whilst also one which work psychologists will frequently perform. Outsourcing of services can impact efficiencies and communication within an organisation as individual contractors understand less about an organisation which they work at a distance from. At the same time flatter structures can make it more difficult for internal promotions as there is greater distance and differences in task at each level. This can be problematic for businesses who lose good employers to competitors as they move to advance to another level. Within some sectors employees can stepping-stone up, backwards and forwards between competitors. This increases organisations' costs as new employees are not as productive until they are fully embedded, and there may also be gaps in service coverages as employees leave. Work psychologists can help with this issue by designing in training routes, structuring career paths and supporting individuals to actively manage their careers.

POLARISATION OF JOBS

Another major change in developed economies is that there has been a decline in manufacturing roles and middle-level jobs. There has been increased automation of jobs requiring a year or less of training coupled with a growth in jobs requiring very little training such as service sector and care roles. It is important to note here that these are sometimes termed low-skills jobs, and a work psychologist should be highly aware that all jobs require skill, some are just lower paid because many more people are able to do the role with minimal training to get started. The terminology low-skills and high-skills job belies the status given to different types of work; some have considerably more status than others. Jobs in the middle have increasingly been taken over by mechanisation or outsourcing to countries with cheaper labour costs. Some cannot be outsourced, for example, care roles and so they remain, and indeed have grown in number. Others are too complicated to mechanise, such as delivery workers. This means that there is an increasing gap between people who have highly marketable skills and qualifications and those who do not. There is less potential for people to move up the ranks of an organisation, and there are both psychological and societal impacts as the two types of employees become further apart. It means that some are likely to be unemployed or underemployed for large portions of their working lives, or in low-paid work. This can have impacts for mental wellbeing, physical health and life chances both for themselves and their children. Work psychologists can work to build policies and systems to mitigate these issues as well as working with individuals themselves to ensure the effects of unemployment or underemployment are less harmful to their mental health.

EFFECT OF COVID PANDEMIC – WORK ISOLATION

The Covid pandemic is an example of the uncertainty element of the VUCA concept: an event that few predicted and had serious impacts on whole populations as well as on how businesses operated. Some of the work effects were immediate, such as the need to shield certain employees and gaps left as some employees died or were left permanently disabled. Some effects resulted from changes in work practices such as shifts to online work and loss of some job roles. Work psychologists had to mobilise quickly to support organisations in building new systems, considering the psychological implications of the new processes and ways of working. They needed to consider how to keep staff engaged and motivated whilst at a distance. The effects of Covid on employees was rapid. Andel et al. (2021) reported how the combination of job insecurity, distance working and uncertainty about outcomes led to work loneliness in the early stages of the pandemic. Work psychologists should note that during uncertain events such as this the organisation itself needs to play a role in providing information, encouraging kindness towards themselves and others as well as a sense of having a shared experience. There is significant evidence to show that self-compassion is important in such situations and that organisational citizenship behaviours become increasingly important at these times. This is important to bear in mind in relation to longer-term working relationships. As we have already seen in Chapter 6 such OCBs are reduced if employees have a transactional relationship with their organisation. The initial loneliness may have stemmed from multiple causes in this pandemic. However, work psychologists need to be mindful that large numbers of roles remained online, or partially online. This move to distance working, coupled with fragmented teams, may have longer-term impacts on work loneliness and isolation. It may also affect sense of belonging or engagement to an organisation and raises problems for how jobs and teams are designed.

THE GREAT RESIGNATION

Another response to the changes brought about by Covid is that people have thought much more about what motivates them, how valued they are as workers, and how they want to engage with work moving forwards. Many furloughed workers had opportunities to engage in hobbies and live differently during this time and wanted to change more permanently as a result. This is not a new phenomenon, but the pandemic accentuated existing patterns of change in culture. This effect has been presented as a backlash against the culture of 'greed is good' which was at its height in the 1980s. Individuals have contributed to hashtags such as #quitmyjob and #anti-ambition, and there has been much discussion of stopping what is termed 'grind culture'. There have been many opinion pieces written about the Great Resignation, pointing out that there were increased numbers of people who chose to retire during the pandemic and others who simply resigned. In particular, concerns have been raised about loss of academics, knowledge workers and healthcare workers. Both the American Hospital Association and British Medical Association have raised concerns about ongoing and predicted future shortages of all medical workers especially doctors. Whilst this is an interesting phenomenon it is important to pull apart resignations which were essentially one-off incidents, early retirements, for example, and an ongoing issue. Most people who resign are going on to other work. Most resignations represent normal movement from one job to another, and the US-based Society for Human Resource Management publishes monthly statistics which illustrate that whilst resignation rates raised rapidly through the furlough period and continued to rise afterwards, the rate has slowed and that currently monthly only about 3% of US workers resign, mostly to go to other jobs. It is not necessarily an issue if older workers choose earlier retirement: the opposite trend has been causing issues of youth unemployment in the recent past. However, this process is problematic if it is sudden and unplanned, especially for highly trained roles, such as doctors, as there have to be replacement plans spanning years to cover their loss. It is vital for work psychologists not to be too alarmed by the Great Resignation, but individual sectors or organisations may experience problems and need to put in place contingency plans.

THE FOUR-DAY WEEK MOVEMENT

Simultaneously with the great resignation movement there have been opposing movements to take up a 'side hustle' a euphemism, often simply meaning a second, third or fourth job, but portrayed as clever entrepreneurialism. The narrative spun around this is that working hard (many hours) is not just necessary to be successful, but it is intrinsically a good thing to do. Again, this is not a new narrative, and it has had other names over time, notably the Protestant work ethic – an idea that it is godly to work hard. It is important that work psychologists engage with these narratives and think about whose interests they serve. Who might want to encourage people to be working extended hours and what has this book taught us so far about the dangers of overwork? Usually work psychologists are hired by senior managers who hope they will improve organisational efficiencies. Ideally those efficiencies should come from reduction in unnecessary actions, more motivated workers and better systems. They should not come from encouraging people to work more. The four-day work week epitomises these principles. The idea, already embedded in Iceland and currently being trialled in the UK, is simple. Advocates argue that people have normalised a five-day working week and there is no particular need to do that. Research demonstrates people are happier, more fit and more engaged when they work four days, it is simply that they cannot always afford to do this. The four-day week movement argues organisations should continue to pay the same salaries for fewer hours and should develop systems, so they are more efficient to make up the extra hours. Trials have been extensive, across a range of industries, and have demonstrated that such a working week is beneficial for both employees and organisations. It is a perfect example of how work psychologists can support organisations to improve whilst also making individual employees lives better.

LOOKING FORWARDS: THE FUTURE OF WORK PSYCHOLOGY

Some of the issues discussed so far in this chapter will continue to have prominence for how work psychologists practise in the coming decades. In addition, there are a range of other issues which are likely to impact in the future, as well. This section firstly explores issues which directly impact the tasks work psychologists will do and then looks at issues impacting how work psychologists will operate, before finally laying out some broader themes which will impact workforces moving forwards.

NEW TASKS FOR WORK PSYCHOLOGISTS

Some of the tasks which will be core to the work are already peripheral elements. Many work psychologists already undertake career counselling, and there is increasing crossover between coaching psychology and therapeutic work. It is important that all psychologists operate within their own specialisms, but with the rise of online and virtual coaching there is a real issue with the lines of these two different areas of work becoming blurred. It is probable that this will become a larger part of the role of work psychologist.

Another developing field is in assisting organisations with specific forms of change management, in particular technology usage and increased globalisations. Again, some psychologists already work with organisations on human–machine interaction issues, but there are increased and changing roles for this type of work as more staff work at a distance and need to use technological tools to support that. They may be supporting organisations to ensure that the benefits of technology usage are balanced against the needs to protect confidentiality of data and ensure that employees maintain feelings of connectedness to each other and build and maintain effective networks. It is probable that managing distance work will become more core in work design. In relation to globalisation, emerging work fields include supporting expatriation assignments. Work psychologists can help organisations choose the right employees to undertake foreign postings, support them in preparing to go and in repatriating them and dealing with culture shock and reverse culture shock when they return. They may also be supporting team building cross-culturally and with teams who are working in different time zones and locations.

Finally, it is probable work psychologists will become much more involved in consumer psychology in particular customer relationship management (CRM). They may be doing tasks such as advising on best practice, assessing employees so that they can be most effectively matched to customers or clients. Consumer psychology became part of the BPS-approved curriculum in their last rewrite, so many newly qualified work psychologists have training in this area. As well as CRM, consumer psychology includes looking at how people make decisions, how they can be rewarded and what influences them. Currently these tasks sit more within marketing functions, but it is probable work psychologists will also support these in the future, with their unique knowledge of human behaviours.

HOW WORK PSYCHOLOGISTS PRACTISE

Work psychologists are workers themselves and as such are not immune to the changes impacting other employees. They are already seeing a shift to more online work themselves, and it is likely this will increase over time. One reason for this is cost savings in distance work; equally it allows work psychologists to work transnationally though. As other employees are working across borders, so too will work psychologists.

An underpinning principle of work psychology is that they should be helping employees, and so in that respect it is a values-driven profession. This can create some tensions as the actual employing client may be, for example, seeking simply to make employees work harder or longer. Looking forwards, values are becoming more important in other areas of work, with millennials choosing to work, or refusing work, with companies based on organisational values. The rise of green human resource management (HRM) may have impacts on the ways in which work psychologists practise too. Green HRM is a research area focused on making working practices more sustainable and environmentally friendly. This is something more consistent with younger workers' views. As such, it is likely that it will impact how work psychologists conduct their interventions, what they advise and how they work.

FUTURE ISSUES IMPACTING WORKPLACES

Finally, we consider what issues are likely to be impactful for all businesses in the future. According to Bakhshi et al.'s (2017) report there are a range of trends which we can expect to see impacting the future of work. Some we have already addressed here such as technological advances, demographic changes and globalisation. They highlight others, which are both related to these and independently impactful. These include growing environmental issues, caused in part by climate change, urbanisation and political uncertainty. These issues collectively are then predicted to lead to increasing inequality, which impacts who works, what resources they have to support them, what they are paid and where, globally, there will be unemployment and underemployment. Bakhshi et al. suggest that employees are going to have to develop different skills to accommodate these effects, broadly these are communication skills, learning skills and thinking skills. Communication skills refers to the ability to collaborate effectively with others, understand them as well as to be able to teach others. Learning skills include the ability to set goals, identify relevant questions and access and respond to feedback. Finally the thinking skills refers to higher-order skills, incorporating active learning from all situations, complex problem-solving skills, creativity in idea formation, judgement and decision-making.

SUMMARY

This chapter brought together the themes underpinning the rest of the book, and how work psychologists practise, before exploring how current changes and future changes are likely to impact what work psychology looks like. Moving forwards work psychologists will continue to operate in the main five domains: psychological assessment at work; learning, training and development; wellbeing; workplace design; and leadership, engagement and motivation. However they are also likely to develop new areas of practice more focused on consumer psychology and technology usage, and perhaps on, as yet, unknown specialisations. The role is already broad, and many work psychologists specialise within the profession. It is probable that there is increased specialisation over time as workplace efficacy and wellbeing are increasingly recognised as the drivers for business success. Work psychologists are likely to be in more demand as workplaces and organisations become increasingly complex. Psychologists, of all types, are in growing demand as the profession is embraced by more countries. Countries which previously have not had this discrete role are now training up their graduates. India and China are notable examples, with many new undergraduate courses opening over the last decade. This helps business leaders to recognise the role psychology can play, which then drives future demand. The future is bright for work psychologists.

RECOMMENDATIONS FOR FURTHER READING

Hopefully this book has whetted your appetite for specialising into this area of psychology. If so, it is important that you keep up to date with current research and theories. The following journals will be particularly helpful in this, as they publish the cutting edge of work psychology advances:

- *Journal of Occupational and Organizational Psychology (usually abbreviated to JOOP)*
- *Journal of Applied Psychology*
- *Applied Psychology: An International Review*
- *Organizational Behavior and Human Decision Processes*
- *Personnel Psychology*
- *Human Relations*
- *Work and Stress*
- *European Journal of Work and Organizational Psychology*
- *Journal of Vocational Behavior.*

In addition, there are some practitioner-focused journals which will be of interest to you in applying this published research. In particular, readers are directed to the *Industrial-Organizational Psychologist* and the new DOP publication *Occupational Psychology Outlook* which is a redesigned version of their long-standing journal.

GLOSSARY

BPS British Psychological Society, the UK based practitioner body for psychologists

Burnout a state of exhaustion and emotional distance from one's job role resulting from chronic stress

Chartership the informal name given to the Stage 2 qualification to qualify as a Chartered Psychologist in the UK.

Constructive alignment a teaching design in which learning tasks and assessments directly relate to the learning outcomes.

CWBs counterproductive work behaviours are deliberate actions which harm a company, for example theft, sabotage, or absenteeism.

EAWOP European Association of Work and Organizational Psychology, a practitioner organisation for work psychologists in Europe.

Extinction loss of skills or knowledge which is not actively used.

Fidelity the extent to which a simulation or proxy reflects the simulated action or behaviour.

Graduate Basis for Registration sometimes abbreviated to GBR is a threshold level of competency, accredited by the BPS as showing sufficient existing training to continue onto training leading to Chartership in the UK. It is usually granted by graduating from a BPS accredited undergraduate degree.

HCPC Health and Care Professions Council, the UK body regulating psychologists

Longitudinal a form of research which has multiple data collection points over time, usually over years, used to establish cause and effect relationships.

Mediation where one variable accounts for the relationship between two other variables.

Moderation where a third variable changes the relationship between two other variables.

MOOCs Massive Open Online Courses are those which have no limit on numbers of participants and are usually delivered at no cost to participants.

Occupational Psychologist a protected title used in the UK for those who have achieved Chartership with the BPS.

Organisational analysis a structured process for appraising systems, processes and operations of a company.

Organisational citizenship behaviours often abbreviated to OCBs these refer to the everyday tasks which facilitate good working but rarely fit explicitly into a job description. Examples might be proofreading a colleague's report, replacing a toner cartridge or buddying a new employee.

Person analysis a step of training needs analysis in which who needs training is identified.

Positive discrimination the process by which underrepresented groups are given advantages in a selection process. (NB, this is illegal throughout the European Union and most other countries).

Practitioner Psychologist the legally protected term which can be used by any psychologist, of any subbranch, who is registered with the HCPC as Chartered.

Psychological Contact the beliefs, expectations and obligations an individual perceives themselves to have agreed implicitly with their employing organisation.

Psychometrics tools designed to assess psychological aspects of an individual. In an occupational psychology context these typically assess ability, personality, motivations, or attitudes.

Qualitative measurement that considers how the subjective qualities of a variable changes.

Quantitative measurement that considers how the objective number of a variable changes.

Relational Contract a type of psychological contract in which the employee trusts their employing organisation.

Reliability the degree to which a finding is consistent.

SIOP Society for Industrial and Organizational Psychologists, a subdivision of the American Psychological Association, an organisation for psychologists.

Task analysis a step of training needs analysis in which the sub elements of work required to complete given tasks are analysed.

Training Needs Analysis sometimes abbreviated to TNA, it is the process of investigating what training and development is needed for future organisation success.

Transactional Contract a type of psychological contract in which the employee negotiates explicitly with their employing organisation, not relying on goodwill or trust.

Validity the degree to which a measurement actually assesses that which it purports to measure.

BIBLIOGRAPHY

Aalto, A. M., Heponiemi, T., Josefsson, K., Arffman, M., and Elovainio, M. (2018). Social relationships in physicians' work moderate relationship between workload and wellbeing—9-year follow-up study. *European Journal of Public Health*.

Adams, J. B., and Miller, R. B. (2008). Bridging psychology's scientist vs. practitioner divide: Fruits of a twenty-five year dialogue. *Journal of Theoretical and Philosophical Psychology, 28*(2), 375.

Adams, J. S. (1963) Toward an understanding of inequity. *Journal of Abnormal and Social Psychology*, 67, 422–436.

Adams, J.S. (1965). Inequity in social exchange. In L.Berkowitz (Ed.), *Advances in experimental social psychology*. Vol. 2, 267–299.

Alavi, S., Abd. Wahab, D., Muhamad, N., and Arbab Shirani, B. (2014). Organic structure and organisational learning as the main antecedents of workforce agility. *International Journal of Production Research, 52*(21), 6273–6295.

Alderfer, C. P. (1972). *Existence, relatedness, and growth: Human needs in organizational settings*. Free Press: Cambridge.

Andel S. A., Shen W., Arvan M. L. (2021). Depending on your own kindness: The moderating role of self-compassion on the within-person consequences of work loneliness during the COVID-19 pandemic. *Journal of Occupational Health Psychology*, 26(4), 276–290

Arthur, W., Jr, Bennet., W. Jr., Stanush, P. and McNelly, T. (1998). Factors that influence skill decay and retention: A quantitative review and analysis. *Human Performance*, 11, 57–101.

Avey, J. B., Luthans, F., Smith, R. M., and Palmer, N. F. (2010). Impact of positive psychological capital on employee well-being over time. *Journal of occupational health psychology, 15*(1), 17.

Bakhshi, H., Downing, J., Osborne, M. and Schneider, P. (2017). *The Future of Skills: Employment in 2030.* London: Pearson and Nesta

Bakker, A. B., Demerouti, E., and Sanz-Vergel, A. I. (2014). Burnout and work engagement: The JD–R approach. *Annual Review of Organisational Psychology and Organisational Behaviour, 1*(1), 389–411.

Bakker, A.B. and Demerouti, E. (2007), "The Job Demands-Resources model: state of the art", *Journal of Managerial Psychology*, Vol. 22 No. 3, pp. 309–328.

Baldwin, S. (2006). *Organisational justice.* Brighton: Institute for Employment Studies.

Bamford, D. R., and Forrester, P. L. (2003). Managing planned and emergent change within an operations management environment. *International Journal of Operations and Production Management.*

Bartlett, D., and Francis-Smythe, J. (2016). Bridging the divide in work and organizational psychology: evidence from practice. *European Journal of Work and Organizational Psychology, 25*(5), 615–630.

Beham, B., Drobnič, S., Präg, P., Baierl, A., and Eckner, J. (2018). Part-time work and gender inequality in Europe: a comparative analysis of satisfaction with work–life balance. *European Societies*, 1–25.

Bernerth, J., Armenakis, A., Feild, H., and Walker, H. (2007). Justice, cynicism, and commitment: A study of important organizational change variables. *The Journal of Applied Behavioral Science, 43*(3), 303–326.

Bishop, S., Lau, M., Shapiro, S., Carlson, L., Anderson, N., Carmody, J.,... and Devins, G. (2004). Mindfulness: a proposed operational definition. *Clinical Psychology: Science and Practice, 11*(3), 230.

Blume, B., Ford, J., Baldwin, T., and Huang, J. (2010). Transfer of Training: A Meta-Analytic Review. *Journal of Management*, 36, 1065–1105.

Blume, B., Ford, J., Baldwin, T., and Huang, J. (2010). Transfer of Training: A Meta-Analytic Review. *Journal of Management*, 36, 1065–1105.

Boy, G. A. (Ed.). (2017). *The Handbook Of Human-Machine Interaction: A Human-Centered Design Approach.* CRC Press.

Briner, R. B., Denyer, D., and Rousseau, D. M. (2009). Evidence-based management: Concept clean-up time? *Academy of Management Perspectives*, 23, 19–32.

British Psychological Society. (2012). *Expert Panel to Review the Future Education and Curriculum for Occupational Psychologists A DOP Report.* British Psychological Society: London.

Burnes, B. (2004). Emergent change and planned change–competitors or allies? The case of XYZ construction. *International Journal of Operations and Production Management*, 24(9), 886–902.

Burnes, B. (2004). *Managing change: A strategic approach to organisational dynamics*. Pearson Education.

Cascio, W. F., and Aguinis, H. (2008). Research in industrial and organizational psychology from 1963 to 2007: Changes, choices, and trends. *Journal of Applied Psychology*, 93, 1062–1081.

Cassell, C., and Symon, G. (Eds.). (2004). *Essential guide to qualitative methods in organizational research*. sage.

Chapman and Zweig (2005). Developing a nomological network for interview structure: Antecedents and consequences of the structured selection interview. *Personnel Psychology, 58*(3), 673–702.

Chonko, L. B., and Jones, E. (2005). The need for speed: Agility selling. *Journal of Personal Selling and Sales Management, 25*(4), 371–382.

CIPD (2021). *Learning and Skills at Work Survey 2021*. CIPD: London

CIPD (2021). *Learning and Skills at Work Survey 2021*. CIPD: London

Cobb, A., Folger, R., and Wooten, K. (1995). The role justice plays in organizational change. *Public Administration Quarterly*, 19(2), 135–151.

Collinson, D. (1994). Strategies of resistance: power, knowledge and subjectivity in the workplace.

Colquitt, J. LePine, J., and Noe, R. (2000). Toward an integrative theory of training motivation; A meta-analytic path analysis of 20 years of research. Journal of Applied Psychology, 85, 678–707.

Coolican, H. (2017). *Research methods and statistics in psychology*. Psychology Press: London

Cortina, J. M., Aguinis, H., and DeShon, R. P. (2017). Twilight of dawn or of evening? A century of research methods in the Journal of Applied Psychology. *Journal of Applied Psychology, 102*(3), 274.

Cottingham, M. D., Erickson, R. J., and Diefendorff, J. M. (2015). Examining men's status shield and status bonus: How gender frames the emotional labor and job satisfaction of nurses. *Sex Roles, 72*(7–8), 377–389.

Csikszentmihalyi, M., and Seligman, M. (2000). Positive psychology. *American Psychologist, 55*(1), 5–14.

Dane, E. (2011). Paying attention to mindfulness and its effects on task performance in the workplace. *Journal of management, 37*(4), 997–1018.

Davies, I. (1972). *The Management of Learning*. London: McGraw-Hill.

Derks, D., van Duin, D., Tims, M., and Bakker, A. B. (2015). Smartphone use and work–home interference: The moderating role of social norms and employee work engagement. *Journal of Occupational and Organizational Psychology, 88*(1), 155–177.

Dhuey, E., Figlio, D., Karbownik, K. and Roth, J., (2017). *School Starting Age and Cognitive Development, Working Paper 23660*. Cambridge, MA: National Bureau of Economic Research

Diener, E., and Suh, M. (1997). Subjective well-being and age: An international analysis. *Annual Review of Gerontology and Geriatrics, 17*(1), 304–324.

Donovan, J. And Dwight, S. (2014). The impact of applicant faking on selection measures, hiring decisions and employee performance. *Journal of Business Psychology, 29*, 479–493.

Dutschke, G., Jacobsohn, L., Dias, A. and Combadão, J. (2019), "The job design happiness scale (JDHS)", *Journal of Organizational Change Management*, 32 (7), 709–724.

Edmonds, J. (2011) "Managing successful change", *Industrial and Commercial Training*, 43(6), 349–353

Eikhof, R. (2007), "Introduction: What work? What life? What balance? Critical reflections on the work-life balance debate", *Employee Relations*, 29(4), 325–333.

Fiedler, F. (1967). *A Theory of Leadership Effectiveness*. New York: McGraw-Hill.

French, W., and Bell, C. (1995). *Organization development: Behavioral science interventions for organization improvement*. Pearson Education: New York.

Fugate, M., Prussia, G., and Kinicki, A. (2012). Managing employee withdrawal during organizational change: The role of threat appraisal. *Journal of Management, 38*(3), 890–914.

Garman, A. N. (2011). Shooting for the moon: How academicians could make management research even less irrelevant. *Journal of Business and Psychology*, 26, 129–133

Gobel, S. (2000). Klaus B: The success story of an entrepreneur-a case study. *European Journal of Work and Organizational Psychology, 9*(1), 89–92.

Goldstein, I and Ford, J. (2001). Training in Organizations: Needs Assessment Development and Evaluation (4th Ed). Belmont, CA: Wadsworth Publishing Co.

Greenberg, J. (1982). Approaching equity and avoiding inequity in groups and organizations. In J. Greenberg and R.L. Cohen (Eds.), *Equity and justice in social behaviour*. 337–351. New York: Academic Press.

Hackman, J. R., and Oldham, G. R. (1976). Motivation through the design of work: Test of a theory. *Organizational Behavior and Human Performance, 16*(2), 250–279.

Hattie, J. (1987). Identifying the salient facets of a model of student learning: a synthesis of meta-analyses. *International Journal of Educational Research*, 11, 187–212.

Hatum, A., and Pettigrew, A. M. (2006). Determinants of organizational flexibility: a study in an emerging economy. *British journal of management*, 17(2), 115–137.

Hermans, H. (1970). A questionnaire measure of achievement motivation. *Journal of Applied Psychology, 54*(4), 353–363.

Herzberg, F. (1959). *The Motivation to Work*. Wiley: New York.

Herzberg, F., Mausner, B., And Snyderman, B. (1959). The Motivation to Work (2nd Ed). New York: John Wiley and Sons.

Hilbert, J., Russ-Eft, D. and Preskill, H. (1997). Evaluating training. In D. Russ-Eft (Ed). *What Works: Assessment, Development and Measurement* (pp 109–150). Alexandria, VA: ASTD

Hodgkinson, G., and Herriot, P. (2002). The role of psychologists in enhancing organizational effectiveness. In Robertson, I., Callinan, M., and Bartram, D. *Organizational Effectiveness: The Role of Psychology*, (pp 45–60). Wiley: New York

House, R. (1971). A path goal theory of leader effectiveness. *Administrative Science Quarterly*, 16(3), 321–339.

House, R.J., Shane, S.A., & Herold, D.M. (1996). Rumors of the death of dispositional research are vastly exaggerated. *Academy of Management Review, 21,* 203–224.

Huffcutt, A. and Arthur, W. (1994): Hunter and Hunter (1984) Revisited: Interview validity for entry level jobs. *Journal of Applied Psychology, 79,* 184–190.

Humphrey, S., Nahrgang, J., and Morgeson, F. (2007). Integrating motivational, social, and contextual work design features: a meta-analytic summary and theoretical extension of the work design literature. *Journal of Applied Psychology, 92*(5), 1332–1356.

Jencks, C., and Phillips, M. (2011). *The Black-White Test Score Gap.* Brookings Institution Press: Washington DC.

Johnson, R. B., and Onwuegbuzie, A. J. (2004). Mixed methods research: A research paradigm whose time has come. *Educational Researcher, 33*(7), 14–26.

Judge, T. A., Heller, D., and Mount, M. K. (2002). Five-factor model of personality and job satisfaction: a meta-analysis.

Kahn, W. A. (1990). Psychological conditions of personal engagement and disengagement at work. *The Academy of Management Journal, 33*(4), 692–724.

Katz, B., and Kahn, R. (1966). The Social Psychology of Organizations. New York: Wiley.

Kelliher, C., and Anderson, D. (2010). Doing more with less? Flexible working practices and the intensification of work. *Human relations, 63*(1), 83–106.

Kiggundu, M. N. (1981). Task interdependence and the theory of job design. *Academy of Management Review*, 6, 499 –508.

Kiken, L., Lundberg, K., and Fredrickson, B. (2017). Being Present and Enjoying It: Dispositional Mindfulness and Savoring the Moment Are Distinct, Interactive Predictors of Positive Emotions and Psychological Health. *Mindfulness*, 8(5), 1290-1290.

Kirkpatrick, D. (1994) *Evaluating Training Programs: The Four Levels.* San Francisco: Berrett-Koehler.

Landers, R. and Schmidt, G. (2016). *Social Media in Employee Selection and Recruitment*. Springer: Switzerland.

Lawshe, C., Bolda, R., Brune, R. and Auclair. G. (1958). Expectancy Charts II. Their Theoretical Development. *Personnel Psychology, 11*(4), 545–559

Li, S., Easterby-Smith, M., and Bartunek, J. (2009). Research methods for organizational learning: The transatlantic gap. *Management Learning, 40*(4), 439–447.

Locke, E. (1976). The nature and causes of job satisfaction. In M. Dunnette (Ed.), *Handbook of industrial and organizational psychology* (pp. 1297–1349). Chicago: Rand McNally.

Locke, E., and Latham, G. (1990). *A Theory of Goal Setting and Task Performance*. Englewood Cliffs, NJ: Prentice-Hall.

Luthans, F., Avolio, B., Avey, J., and Norman, S. (2007). Positive psychological capital: Measurement and relationship with performance and satisfaction. *Personnel Psychology, 60*(3), 541–572.

Marks, N., and Shah, H. (2004). A well-being manifesto for a flourishing society. *Journal of Public Mental Health, 3*(4), 9–16.

Martins, L. (2011). Organizational change and development. In *APA Handbook of Industrial and Organizational Psychology, Vol 3: Maintaining, Expanding, and Contracting The Organization*. (pp. 691–728). American Psychological Association: Washington, DC.

Maslach, C. and Jackson, S. (1986). *MBI: The Maslach Burnout Inventory: Manual Research Edition*. Consulting Psychologists Press, Palo Alto, CA.

Maslow, A. (1943). A theory of human motivation. *Psychological Review, 50,*4, 370–396.

Mathieu, J., and Zajac, D. (1990). A review and meta-analysis of the antecedents, correlates, and consequences of organizational commitment. *Psychological Bulletin, 108*(2), 171–194.

McClelland, D. (1961). *The Achieving Society*. Van Nostrand: New York.

McCormick, D., and Hunter, J. (2008). Mindfulness in the Workplace: An Exploratory Study. In *Academy of Management Annual Meeting, Annaheim, California*.

Moran, J., and Brightman, B. (2001). Leading organizational change. *Career Development International, 6*(2), 111–119.

Morgeson, F., and Humphrey, S. (2006). The Work Design Questionnaire (WDQ): developing and validating a comprehensive measure for assessing job design and the nature of work. *Journal of Applied Psychology, 91*(6), 1321.

Muduli, A. (2015). High performance work system, HRD climate and organisational performance: an empirical study. *European journal of Training and development*, 39(3):239–257

Noon M (2010). The shackled runner: time to rethink positive discrimination? *Work, Employment and Society* vol. 24, (4) 728–739.

Oldham, G., Hackman, J., and Pearce, J. (1976). Conditions under which employees respond positively to enriched work. *Journal of Applied Psychology, 61*(4), 395–403.

Organ, D. W. (1988). *Organizational Citizenship Behavior: The Good Soldier Syndrome.* Lexington Books: Lanham, Maryland.

Overell, S. (2009). Inwardness: The rise of meaningful work. *Provocation Series,* 4(2). The Work Foundation: London

Pidd, K. (2004). The impact of workplace support and identity on training transfer: a case study of drug and alcohol safety training in Australia. *International Journal of Training and Development, 8*(4), 274–288.

Piderit, S. K. (2000). Rethinking resistance and recognizing ambivalence: A multidimensional view of attitudes toward an organizational change. *Academy of Management Review, 25*(4), 783–794.

Pieterse, J. H., Caniëls, M. C., and Homan, T. (2012). Professional discourses and resistance to change. *Journal of Organizational Change Management.*

Richard, P., Devinney, T., Yip, G., and Johnson, G. (2009). Measuring organizational performance: Towards methodological best practice. *Journal of Management, 35*(3), 718–804.

Robbins, S., and Judge, T. (2017). *Essentials of Organizational Behavior,* Pearson Press: London.

Rousseau, D. (1990). New Hire Perceptions of their Own and Their Employer's Obligations: A Study of Psychological Contracts, *Journal of Organizational Behaviour,* 11, 389–400.

Rudolph. C., Katz, I., Lavigne, K., and Zacher, H. (2017). Job crafting: a meta-analysis of relationships with individual differences, job characteristics, and work outcomes. *Journal of Vocational Behavior,* 102, 112–138

Ryan, A. and Ployhart, R. (2014). A century of selection. *Annual Review of Psychology,* 65, 693–717.

Ryan, M.and Haslam, S. (2007). The glass cliff: Exploring the dynamics surrounding women's appointment to precarious leadership positions. *Academy of Management Review, 32,* 549–572.

Salas, E., Tannenbaum, S., Kraiger, K. and Smith-Jentsch, K. (2012). The science of training and development in organisations: What matters in practice. *Psychological Science in the Public Interest, 13,* 74–101.

Schaufeli, W., Bakker, A., and Salanova, M. (2006). The measurement of work engagement with a short questionnaire: A cross-national study. *Educational and Psychological Measurement, 66*(4), 701–716.

Schaufeli, W., Salanova, M., Gonzalez-Roma, V., and Bakker, A. (2002). The measurement of engagement and burnout: A two sample confirmatory factor analytic approach. *Journal of Happiness Studies, 3,* 71–92.

Schein, E. H. (1985). Defining organizational culture. *Classics of Organization Theory, 3*(1), 490–502.

Schein, V. (1973). The relationship between sex role stereotypes and requisite management characteristics. *Journal of Applied Psychology, 57*, pp. 95–105.

Schippmann, J., Ash, R., Battista, M., Carr, L., Eyde, L., Hesketh, B., et al. (2000). The practice of competency modeling. *Personnel Psychology, 53*, 703–740.

Schmidt, F., and Hunter, J. (1998). The validity and utility of selection methods in personnel psychology: Practical and theoretical implications of 85 years of research findings. *Psychological Bulletin, 124*, (2), 262–274.

Selye, H. (1974). *Stress without Distress.* Philadelphia: Lippincott

Shin, D., and Johnson, D. (1978). Avowed happiness as an overall assessment of the quality of life. *Social Indicators Research, 5*(1), 475–492.

Silzer, R., Cober, R., Erickson, A., Robinson, G. (2008). *Practitioner Needs Survey: Final Survey Report.* Society for Industrial and Organizational Psychology: Bowling Green, Ohio.

Sitzman, T. and Ely, K. (2011). A meta-analysis of self-regulated learning in work-related training and educational attainment: What we know and where we need to go. *Psychological Bulletin, 137*, 421–42.

Skirbekk, V. (2004). Age and individual productivity: A literature survey. *Vienna Yearbook of Population Research, 1*, 133–153.

Somaieh A., Dzuraidah A., Norhamidi, M. and Behrooz, A. (2014) Organic structure and organisational learning as the main antecedents of workforce agility, *International Journal of Production Research, 52* (21), 6273–6295.

Stoughton, A., and Ludema, J. (2012). The driving forces of sustainability. *Journal of Organizational Change Management, 25*(4), 501–517.

Sugrue, B., and Rivera, R. (2005). *ASTD 2005 State of The Industry Report.* American Society for Training and Development: Alexandria, Virginia.

Tatum, C. (1981). New matrix organization for construction manager. *Issues in Engineering Journal of Professional Activities, 107*(4), 255–267.

Taylor, C., Harrison, J., Haimovitz, K., Oberle, E., Thomson, K., Schonert-Reichl, K., and Roeser, R. (2016). Examining ways that a mindfulness-based intervention reduces stress in public school teachers: A mixed-methods study. *Mindfulness, 7*(1), 115–129.

Terpstra, D., Mohammed, A. and Kethley, R. (1999). An analysis of federal court cases, involving nine selection devices. *International Journal of Selection and Assessment, 7*(1), 26–33.

Todnem By, R. (2005). Organisational change management: A critical review. *Journal of change management, 5*(4), 369–380.

Vakola, M. (2014). What's in there for me? Individual readiness to change and the perceived impact of organizational change. *Leadership and Organization Development Journal, 35*(3), 195–209.

Vroom, V., & Yetton, P. (1973). *Leadership and Decision-Making.* Pittsburgh, PA: University of Pittsburgh Press

Vroom, V.H. (1964). *Work and motivation*. New York: Wiley.

Warr, P. (2007a). Learning about employee happiness. *Revista Psicologia Organizações e Trabalho*, 7(2), 133–140.

Warr, P. (2007b). Searching for happiness at work. *The Psychologist*, 20(12):726–729

Warr, P., Bird, M and Rackham, N. (1970). *Evaluation of Management Training: A Practical Framework, with Cases, for Evaluating Training Needs and Results*. London: Gower Press.

Webster, F. (2016). The BMJ should not narrowly confine publication to positivist quantitative studies. *BMJ: British Medical Journal, 352.*

Williams, K., Schaffer, M. and Ellis, L. (2013). Legal risk in selection: an analysis of processes and tools. *Journal of Business Psychology, 28*, 401–410

Willingham, D., Hughes, E. and Dobolyi, D. (2015). The scientific status of learning styles theories. *Teaching of Psychology. 42(3): 266–271.*

Woods, S. and West, M (2010). *Leadership in Organizations*. Sage: London

Yuan, S., Wu, F., and Tang, G. (2018). Work Connectivity, Emotional Exhaustion, Turnover Intention and Work-Life Balance. In *Academy of Management Proceedings* (Vol. 2018, No. 1, p. 17883). Briarcliff Manor, NY 10510: Academy of Management.

INDEX

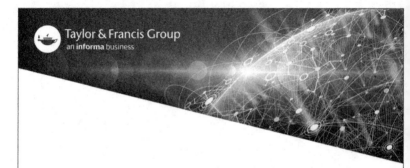

Printed in the United States
by Baker & Taylor Publisher Services